# REAL MEN CRY

## THE DEEP INNER FEELINGS AND THOUGHTS OF A MAN'S MIND, HEART, SOUL AND SPIRIT

---

To Christ Patrol

Thank You For your Great Friend Ship

Charles Merriweather

AKA

## CHARLES MERRIWEATHER

Pastor Majestic

Real Men Cry

Published in the United States
ISBN: 9781513683164



Cover Design: Shekinah Glory Publishing
Editing/Publishing: Shekinah Glory Publishing
Cover Photo Credit: Kenisha Merriweather
Cover Verbiage Credit: Tameka Harty

Shekinah Glory
PUBLISHING

www.shekinahglorypublishing.org

**(936) 314-7458**

# DEDICATION PAGE

This book is dedicated to my mother, Yvonne Merriweather, and my grandmother Sarah Thompson.

# ACKNOWLEDGEMENTS


"A Special Thanks to Special People"

First, I want to start by thanking God for breathing the breath of life into me and allowing me to live these 44 years on the earth. I am grateful for the gift of expression, the gift to listen, and the gift to write. I want to thank God for creating me in His image, for gracing me to be a student of His word, and an instrument to His message.

Finally, I want to thank each of the special people in my life who inspired me to reach my full potential to write this book.

Nadine, Simone, Ashley, my sister Trina, Wanda, Cheyenne, Sharad, Raquel, Reggie, Christina, Jennifer, Caroline, Cisco, Will, Ronald, Alfonso, Melvin, Tony, Demas, Aunt Cathy, Tone, my brother Jarriel, Rah, Rob, Cary, Aaron, Dmitri, Ralah, Merlon, Tamara, Andy, Saprina, Leo, Courteney, Messiah, Yohance, Ev, Ian, Jason, Apostle King Larry, my father Charles, and Kenisha

Thank you all and may God bless each of you!

# TABLE OF CONTENTS

MEN SUFFICATE, IGNORE, SUPRESS, EXPRESS, SUBSTITUTE AND HIDE THEIR FEELINGS THROUGH THE FOLLOWING WAYS:

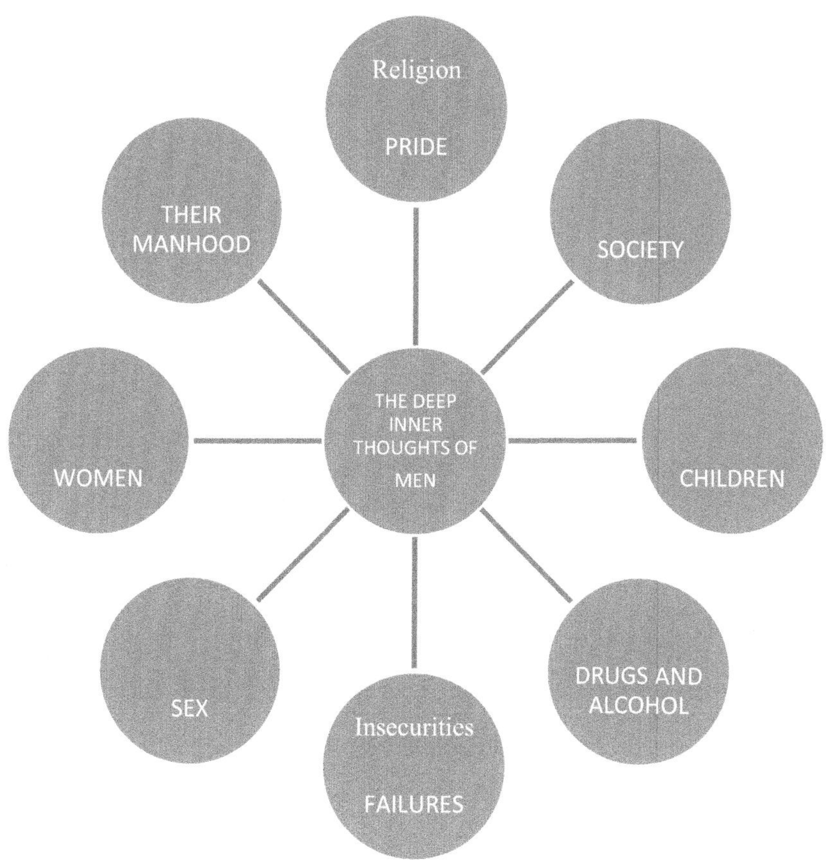


# SPIRITUAL, SOCIAL, AND EMOTIONAL FACTS ABOUT UNRELEASED PAIN

# INTRODUCTION

When I look back over my life. I never in my wildest dreams envisioned writing a book, partially about my life, but most of all about being a man. There were certain things about myself that I began to realize at an early age that guided me to write these words that hadn't yet materialized into expressed thoughts. Thoughts that soon became levels of communication that led me to motivate, entertain, showcase, and enlighten.

My expression of growth began to formulate into a seed that was allowing me to encourage people in ways that even shocked me. There were many who were encouraged and moved to listen. No matter the situation, I was going to tell you what was on my heart and mind! And mind you, I was incredibly young, still trying to figure myself out. To be honest, I wasn't that confident in too many things. I was overly confident in exposing and expressing my feelings to people who would dare to listen to my words.

Growing up as a kid, I looked forward to all the appreciation days or holidays such as, Mother's Day, Valentine's Day, birthday's, etc. These days gave me the opportunity to expose and express the way I felt about my family, friends, or other people I cared about. As I grew older and more mature, I developed a passion for writing and creating deep emotional poems and poetry. Even though I was developing and realizing these gifts and talents, in my heart there was still something missing. I was lacking wisdom, guidance, and direction. My lack of direction and guidance caused me to become impatient, upset and frustrated with not knowing how to utilize these God given abilities.

Eventually I became confused, upset, and uncontrollably bitter. It took some time, but I realized that I was being introduced to the emotional side of myself! If you didn't know, let me be the first to tell you. People who are led by their emotions will find themselves in deep trouble, trying to figure out what's real and what's not. We will discuss the difference between real and fake in more detail throughout the book. Being emotional caused me to lack self-control.

I was unstable, with very minimal direction. There were a series of events that contributed to my instabilities. The very first, was the unfortunate and untimely passing of my mother. Though exceedingly difficult to comprehend, it caused me to seek God wholeheartedly, for the guidance and direction that was missing in my life. My encounter with God during that span, allowed Him to inspire me to write this book. This of course is when I realized that God was that final piece of the puzzle that I was missing. He had the pieces that I needed and through this book I will share how my life has been transformed.

In this book I will deal with several topics relating to men. I believe there are too many men who are afraid, or who live in emotional darkness. For some of us, it is just a matter of expressing ourselves through positive outlets of expression, confession, or humility. Lacking expression and humility can cause us to be blinded to or hide the truth. The expression allows us to get help, because we are now willing to be open and honest. I'm sure you've heard the cliché, "Confession is good for the soul."

Well, it allows us to understand where we are and eventually helps us to learn our true identity in Christ. This will begin to foster a deeper relationship with self and open the doors to have an intimate relationship with God. The first thing we are going to tackle as you read is PRIDE. Pride has caused many men to fail in life. The scriptures tell us that *God resists the proud but gives grace to the humble.* Humility is the key to a balanced and successful life. The humility will destroy or kill the outer pride and destroy the alter ego that is established through hidden or the unreleased pain.

I believe if we focus or concentrate on doing these things more, in no particular order, then we will be more successful in any and everything we do. Then and only then, will we allow ourselves to come closer to the truth (spiritual) about us and closer to the light and, to shine as strong powerful men who are more aware and open. Men who no longer ignore, substitute, suffocate, or hide what they really feel, because they know that the truth of the matter is ***Men Cry Too***, whether it is the same or different, still in all, if you are a man and you are *real* then you will indeed cry, and that sums up the title "Real Men Cry"! Hopefully and respectfully as you read this book, you are and will be inspired, renewed, uplifted, encouraged, if needed reborn, and educated in a way you have never been before.

# CHAPTER ONE

## "Pride Defined"

Did you know there were two different types of pride? One deals with the inner man and the other deals with the outer man. Inner pride focuses on the heart. You witness this pride based on an individual's level of confidence, hard work, and effectiveness. This individual focuses on accomplishments of the mind, heart, and soul that most times allows a man not to just feel good; but be good, regardless of how he's viewed or talked about by others. It doesn't matter how many times he falls he will continuously find joy and be at peace especially during trials and tribulations. This pride is good and healthy. It allows the individual to grow and to be spiritually led.

Outer pride focuses on the opposite. An individual who battles with outer pride is focused more on looking and feeling good. At first glance it can appear to look like inner pride. However, when its challenged, questioned, or embarrassed, outer pride can become negative, bad, or even deadly towards the heart, mind, and soul. It is deadly because it hides the spirit and introduces you to the negative ego. Outer pride is focused on the flesh, people, ego, and money.

An individual operating in this pride doesn't want to look bad. They are always worried about being respected. They live for material things and try to avoid embarrassment and any type of negative energy. These individuals find themselves being continuously hurt, battling depression, living miserably, losing identity, becoming fake, and feeling lost for an extended period.

Many are not aware that the inner and outer pride are interchangeable. There's really no compromise between the two. Either you follow one and, in the process, dismiss or quench the other. Trust me, we are all tempted and tested with one or both, in any and every way possible. The question is, which one will you follow?

## The Prideful Truth

For as long as I can remember, people have told me that a man's greatest weakness is his *big ego*. Others say it's his love for money. Then some say it is envy, hate, or jealousy lingering in his heart. Many might argue that a man's real weakness is a woman. Speaking of women! I asked several of them what they thought about men and pride.

One of the issues acknowledged was the man and his ego, or the fact that men struggle to be good listeners. Another issue was a man's lack of sensitivity. In other words, most men according to them are insensitive, too full of themselves, or both. Now this is a debatable question that can cause some confusion. As men when it comes to addressing the matter of ego, we are told to do some soul searching, which requires focusing on self.

We are told to MAN UP! This can pose a challenge because it is somewhat impossible to soul search and focus on women at the same time. One is going to take precedence over the other. We must take into consideration that the government, social networks, society, and/or different religions or faiths are telling us to define our ego, while others are suggesting we let it go! What's right and what's wrong?

In my opinion, as well as proven facts, we sometimes tend to listen to some outward things that prove to be untrue. I believe a man's greatest weakness is our OUTER Pride, coupled with its twin the Ego. Coincidentally both are influenced, led, and taught by the environment we were reared in or currently reside in. Now, from the woman's point of view a prideful man is full of himself to the point of being self-approved and self-fulfilled. In layman's terms a prideful man is full of himself. This is where the term "*he is prideful*" comes from. His pride is all wrapped up in his outer self!

Most men simply desire to do what makes us look or feel good about ourselves. The truth to some of us is based on the feeling of importance, power, control, or our appearances. No man wants to feel or look bad. Therefore, some men will do whatever it takes to protect his image in front of others. At some point this causes us to follow people and not ourselves, slowly creating a barrier between our true emotions and the outer pride, or the now newly introduced ego.

We will begin to follow whatever the crowd, people, or society is doing, without even realizing it. Some of us allow our outer pride to dictate what we do, where we go, and who we are, simply believing that it's the way to go, or a normality that's natural. The scary part is, we sometimes make such argumentative statements like, "Yo, I'm doing me" or the classic "I don't need nobody."

We feed these statements to the same people we share bills with. The ones who bailed us out of jail. The young lady who we partnered and had our kids with. The one who co-signed our brand-new BMW, helped raised us from birth, fought for us or with us, etc. This is the reality of the mind that is set to believe that this is the proper MINDSET to have, without realizing the compromise and the contradiction it is really displaying!

This helps to prove that most men are full of themselves, confused, arrogant and have big egos. We all must look deep within ourselves to be better. Yet how can we look deep inside of something that we don't know, or something we do know, but are afraid to look at, or that we are in denial about? When approaching this, some of us no longer follow the truth within ourselves. Instead, we follow the lie that has nothing to do with who we really are. Unfortunately, by doing this we become defeated, while being led by the outer to neglect the inner, causing us to erase the truth.

Erasing the truth! What is the truth? The truth is what lies within us, and not him, her, or them. Self-identification is the key to open many things. Especially involving life situations that will challenge our characters and mold our personalities. This can create an ongoing war between the character within that personally competes with the outer, or what the bible refers to as the flesh. Many times, we tend to think we are in competition with something or someone else, not realizing that we are competing against ourselves.

Most men are determined to defeat, destroy, and demolish the competition. When we possess big ego's or outward pride, a huge problem is created if we lose in whatever we are competing with or against. In the event that we lose, our ego and pride cause us to try and figure out what the so-called enemy (our competitors) is doing different from us. We ask questions like, "What are they doing that I'm not?" and "Why are they winning, and I'm losing?"

Without realizing it, we become blind to ourselves trying to figure out the truth of who we are. The true question is, why are we competing in the first place? Why do we feel like it's the end of the world if we lose the battle? Therefore, we must determine who the true enemy is. Are we really fighting against someone else, or are we fighting against our true self? If we are fighting against something or somebody else this really has nothing to do with our true identity, but everything to do with a false identity that we've allowed to take control.

This control thing becomes an ongoing battle that always wants to be in control of a circumstance or situation that is controlled by the now deceptive or carnal mind, and not the heart. If men have established this mentality; then he will live his life accordingly. Therefore, erasing the reality that no one is superior nor perfect and everybody falls. At any time, we can be defeated, broken down, and humbled in life. When a man lacks humility, outer pride takes full control.

Now, for some men it is difficult to accept defeat. Even when we know we've been defeated; we will create excuses for the failure to prevent looking bad in front of others. We do this because it hurts to lose. Most of the time, the things that make us look or feel bad, are indeed true. In this state of mind, we will do anything not to fall or fail, especially if the competition or the next man is winning.

The more the next man wins, the feelings of envy and jealousy begin to fester. If not dealt with, these feelings will eventually turn to hate. Therefore, we use the term or saying, "Don't hate on me!" Fellows this is the outer pride speaking. I don't know about you, but there have been plenty of times, I said I was going to be true to me. This meant I was willing to protect myself and my image by any means necessary. This is important because no one is going to protect us like we protect ourselves.

If we fail or come in second place, many times we are told to try harder or give it another shot next time. This causes a man to feel somewhat irrelevant. This is crushing and damaging to a man's ego, no matter what level he is on in life. This brings me to my next point.

We as men must understand and realize that we should focus inwardly, while accepting and loving ourselves. Once we operate in this manner, it wouldn't matter if we came in second, third, or even tenth place. Because if truth be told, we gave it all we had. This doesn't mean that the other person is better than us. This simply means he was better prepared, trained or taught. It could also be a natural gift for that person. This means we must change our perception from a loss to a win and look at the lesson learned, which is to be better prepared the next time.

But let's be real, we are talking about pride, which tries to tell you that the other person was stronger or better than you. This is that built up insecurity that is attacking your real character and stopping it from growing. As men we must first learn to win, by losing first. The only problem with this is how we allow ourselves to be defined by society.

Sadly, the society we live in judges us based on levels of rings, trophies, degrees, materialism, money status, celebrity status, who we know, or how we look outwardly. So, instead of correcting the problem or understanding it, some of us still try to win, not realizing we were supposed to lose, to learn how to win. Losing keeps us humble, while winning builds outer pride or ego. There's nothing wrong with competing, setting goals to win, striving for the best, or striving for perfection. God created and gave us an ego for His particular purpose.

The problem is, sometimes we use our ego, or allow it to use us for such things like fame, glory, selfishness, etc., and miss Gods intended purpose. Do you know what your purpose is? If you do, that is great and if you don't just keep reading, you will learn more about yourself as you read the remainder of this book. Now we owe it to ourselves to answer some hard questions.

*Why are we competing?*

*Who are we competing against?*

*If we lose, why do we get mad?*

*When we act out in rage, why are we so angry and where is it coming from?*

*Why do we feel like we've lost, even when we've won?*

If we be brutally honest, we know why we feel defeated. These feeling arise when we have possibly cheated, stepped on someone's toes, took a short cut, or know that we are not better than the next man. These feelings are our conscience. The reality that speaks to our true inner hidden emotions. Our conscience becomes the truth of how we really feel despite the outer pride approach. This is a reality that some men are not willing to be honest about. To correct this pride thing, we must first recognize, and realize who we are.

We must listen to our inner spirit that is trying to get our attention instead of ignoring it. We must be willing to follow and listen to that still small voice and not those around us. Then there are those who listen to their inner voice, but the question remains are you hearing the right things? This reminds me of the commercial with the angel on one side and the devil on the other. We are always fighting against more than one opinion. There is the wisdom of God, the thoughts of man and the deceptive truth of the enemy.

We must know the difference in order to see the big picture and have clarity for our lives. This is the only way we will know where to go, how to be, what to follow, and who to listen to based on the truth within ourselves.

By now I'm sure you've recognized just how serious this pride thing really is. This didn't just start; it has been going on since the beginning of time. It's a part of our tradition, culture, and society. We as men are taught to substitute, hide, or ignore that pride exist in our lives. Most of us feel we were born prideful. In another chapter I will share statistics that show the experience of men's emotions.

Many of us have been taught in error, that it's ok to neglect our emotional pain, sadness, insecurities, embarrassment, compassion, or sensitivity to name a few. We compete with ourselves while training the outward not to feel sad, show vulnerability, or any discomfort. The now established outer pride becomes the substitute or the imposter of who we really are and how we really feel. This leads us to believe that it's ok to pretend to be happy. We think it's ok to suppress our feelings and substitute it with material things like money or gambling which is now another added competition.

Some, not all, continue to focus on the outer man who longs for attention. The result of this attention seeking is to get women, abuse alcohol and/or drugs and make money. There are many who can't live without one or all these vices. We will strive to get these things by any means necessary, even if it causes pain and suffering. We convince ourselves that it's okay to become numb. We look good on the outside but feel horrible on the inside, to the point where we can become blind to ourselves.

Since we are on the topic of feelings, many of us have been taught that crying, or showing our emotional side is wrong or weak for men no matter the situation. Therefore, we train ourselves, or become influenced by our family and peers to robotically act or be different. The reality or sad thing is we don't really become different. We establish ego or outer pride and hide how we truly feel. So, instead of following the feeling and defining it by the root, we follow the traditional patterns and cultural teaching that leads us further away from the truth of who we really are and how we really feel.

We are basically told to be fearful individual leaders in society; but we are taught to become followers. So instead of standing out and being different, we are really the same, and are being equally yoked together. It's like a group of men being in the same boat, but all are at the same time trying to paddle in a different direction. Speaking of direction, men and women ask yourself this question! Right now, yeah, it's you I'm talking to, the reader.

*Do you feel like you are truthful to who you are and to the people who truly know or think they know you?*

*Do you even understand what being true to yourself means?*

*Are you keeping it real?*

We will address the *keeping it real* statement later, but right now I need you to ponder the questions. We are the only ones who can truly answer these questions for ourselves. Our answers will determine who we are, and as a result will expose the feelings that sometimes get overlooked, confused, lost, and unable to be manifested because of egotistic pressure we put on ourselves. If we continuously question ourselves, we will slowly begin to realize that the ego, the outer pride, or unnecessary pressure was not caused by you (spiritually) but some sort of false identity outside of who you really are.

If you ask your best friend, your cousin, brother, or your co-worker to describe you, what will they say? To be honest most of us know that their response will be based off what we've shown them. Now what if that same question is posed to your mother, grandmother, wife, girlfriend, or somebody who's known you your whole life. If they are asked to describe your character, personality etc., would it be different than the first group of people who were asked? If the answer is yes, then the next question would be which description is real?

# CHAPTER TW

## "Externally Destroyed Pride"

Let's look at the movie; Rocky I, where Apollo Creed played by Carl Weather's was the popular black professional boxer who fought the Russian dude, who was a better fighter, more powerful, better trained, and was taking steroids. Then you had, Rocky Balboa, who was of course played by the actor Sylvester Stallone. He was humble, a good fighter, and well trained. Now let me briefly tell you about the movie.

You basically had three professional boxers, and one ring. The Russian guy and Apollo Creed were currently fighting, while Rocky was retired. The Russian came from Russia to challenge and fight Americans. Apollo creed was one of the first fighters to agree to fight this Russian champ. But as we all know, before you can fight, you first need some time to prepare for the fight, and train. Your mind and body need to be worked and thoroughly equipped as possible. Now, Apollo Creed was trained by all of his professional trainers, who were considered the best. While The Russian guy barely trained at all.

After Apollo finished his training, he was finally ready to fight the Russian. Now, keep in mind, before the fight started, Apollo's trainers first told him that the Russians strength was beyond what they ever witnessed before. There were numerous reports that he barely put every guy he fought in the hospital with severe knock outs. They continuously stressed that Apollo had to be fully trained, well prepared, and extremely careful.

In other words, his people pretty much were telling him that he had truly little to no chance of winning. To make a long movie, or a long story short; the day finally came, and it was time for Apollo to fight this steroid taking, well prepared, no mercy, out to kill, Russian fighter. Right before Apollo was to go in the ring, his trainers asked him, was he mentally, emotionally, and physically ready? And of course Apollo said *yeah*, with a fake smile. But deep down inside, he was scared out his mind; another example of keeping it real outwardly, while being fake inwardly.

The truth was, he really wasn't prepared, and he definitely needed more training. The truth of the matter was, all of the training in the world probably would not have prepared, or allowed Apollo to compete with the Russian, who was a big favorite to demolish him. Right before the fight, the last day of the press conference, the Russian told Apollo face to face, that he would kill him. That he had no chance. But Apollo was so focused on looking good, that he faked, and acted foolishly. He was joking and playing all types of games with the Russian and his supporters, to try to take his mind off of the fight itself.

He even acted like he wanted to challenge him before the fight, by antagonizing, embarrassing, disrespecting, and belittling the Russian. He even insulted his wife. Instead of Apollo, taking this fight seriously, and allowing himself to be in control; he was out of control, dancing, singing, and entertaining the crowd, right before the fight. Basically, it was all about the outward appearance, caring about the people, and not caring about his self. He was too focused on what people thought, or felt, instead of his own feelings, or thoughts.

And speaking of thought's, just think about what Apollo Creed said, right before he got knocked out permanently. He told his trainer, or coach, not to stop the fight, even though he wasn't ready to die. He chose his pride, over his own life. There are a lot of lessons about pride to learn from Apollo Creed. One of them is, he allowed himself to be led by his outer pride, instead of his inner. His pride or ego told him to act tough. To act like he can win. He told his coach no matter what don't stop the fight. Is this not a perfect example of outer pride or what!

Deep down on the inside, behind closed doors, he was inwardly scared out of his mind. However, he was arrogant, prideful, and full of himself, cocky and unwise. So instead of expressing once again how he really felt, he only showed his outer and as a result he lost his life in the movie. Now on the other hand, his best friend Rocky, was the complete opposite. His character was, humble, communicative, expressive, wise, and confident. If he was afraid, he was not too afraid to admit it. In fact, he told his trainers, himself, his wife, his son, and even God that he was afraid to fight the Russian.

You see, he was both inwardly and outwardly connected to his feelings. As a result of his feelings, he acted wisely with both. Outwardly he trained hard. He brought his family to train with him, to help and to hold him accountable. At the end of the movie, he beat the Russian guy well.

Even though he got beat beyond recognition. Rocky wasn't afraid to show he was scared, and he came out victorious. But think about it; because he was humbly afraid, that same emotional feeling allowed him to train hard enough to compete at a higher level, so that whether win or lose, he knew deep down inside that he gave it his all. This allowed him to take the good pride in his victory. At the end he cried, and you all know the famous line he said at the end with blood gushing out of his head, "Adrian, Adrian".

Question: Did rocky allow his scared feelings to overtake him? Absolutely not! He did the opposite. Men it's okay to express yourself to whomever you trust. Rocky expressed himself to his wife, his trainers, friends, family, and God. Because he expressed himself, in return, it allowed him to expose his desire, ability, passion, and skills to compete. Even though his competition was overwhelmingly favored, that same favor motivated and inspired him to train and work harder. This allowed him to take good pride in himself, regardless of the outcome.

This movie showed me that real dedication to hard work, to work on oneself inwardly, physically, mentally, and spiritually will all pay off. So, men realize this, in life if you shortchange yourself it will eventually shortchange you! Men work hard continuously, persevere, and be strong. Some of us need to stop allowing our pride to hinder our destiny in life. I can go on and on telling you numerous stories on how I allowed my pride to hide and suffocate my true feelings, but I will probably need twenty more books to explain it all.

I honestly believe that most men want to be humble and allow their true feeling to come out outwardly before it's too late, but as men we are afraid to look bad. We will rather keep it in and hide, than pay for the consequences later on. Sadly, today we are taught that expression and crying out or breaking down is a sign of weakness. I choose to differ. I believe it's a sign of strength. This same strength allows us to surrender to our real feelings, while exposing the truth and the root of them.

Just like Rocky did in the movie, we all can do the same. Understanding and recognizing our emotions is the first step. If needed, expressing, or releasing it is the next one. These two steps are the beginning and the most effective way to handle and deal with it. Understanding our emotions is the key to various positives and exposure to different strengths within.

Life has the potential to bring about sorrow, neglect, hurt, abuse, trauma, pain, suffering, death, and hardship. On the flip side it can produce times filled with laughter, joy, and peace. All of these feelings and emotions pour out from the same heart. Based on society we are supposed to feel like everyone else and release our emotions the same, but this is impossible. Men are not wired the same as women. They were created to be emotional. This is a part of who they are.

When we release emotionally, we must release any and all negative thoughts. We are responsible for clearing our minds, which negatively effects our emotions. We must be willing to do the three R's – Release, React, and Respond.

# CHAPTER THREE

## "Keeping It Real"

We have all heard the famous saying, "Yo, I'm keeping it real!" or "I'm keeping it one hundred!" What does this mean for us as men? Defining this for yourself is very crucial. If you are confused or unsure, let me break it down a little further. Do you need a person, place, material possessions, a title, a label, or thing to identify who you are? If you were not easily identifiable based on these things, would you feel or be lost? If the answer is yes, are you really keeping it real? Now, before you get uptight, hear me out.

Consider the reality that you could be using someone or something to define or identify who you are. When you were first born you were identified as a baby boy or baby girl. Names and titles are used to provide a sense of awareness, acknowledgement, and purpose. They can also provide a sense of importance or belonging. This sense of belonging becomes your personal emotional attachment that begins to create your image, personality, and ego.

Now this created outward name, image, or status allows you to believe that your spirit and heart is the same with it; even though you are really identified by the essence of your already established personality or soul. And of course, you just read about how the mind is the only one or the first one that you are really competing against. Many of us continue to follow the image that slowly causes us to abide by a teaching whether wrong or right. This teaching becomes the norm or false reality of who we are, instead the realness becomes who or what we became.

I say we for the simple fact that we make up the society that we live in. Keeping it real is based on what we were taught. Therefore, the next series of questions will help you to determine what you've been taught in regard to keeping it real.

*What and who directed your steps?*

*Are you following what you see or hear?*

*Do you deceive or lie?*

*Do you manipulate or seek to educate your mind?*

*Is your direction being guided by self, or are you being led by a belief, method, or religion?*

These questions will help to establish your realness based on direction. But then the following questions also need to be considered.

*How are you keeping it real, without a real education?*

*How are you keeping it real if you are hiding behind your feelings?*

*How are you keeping it real if you don't really know how to explain, react, control, or identify your emotions?*

*How are you keeping it real if you really don't have a clue who created you?*

*How are you keeping it real if, you must be fake, in order to be successful?*

*Or better yet how are you keeping it real, with fake people around you?*

Hopefully, by pondering these questions and answering them, you can see yourself in a whole new light. The dictionary defines *keeping it real* as being able to express your feelings, thoughts, attitudes, and emotions regardless of the state of company, circumstance, or situation you are in; regardless of how it may look, be taken or perceived. It basically means to be yourself. To be humble and willing to expose who you are in every aspect of your life. This sounds like the definition of confession and humility to me. I will pose the question once again. Are we really keeping it real?

Don't get me wrong, we all lie, we can be deceitful, and have exaggerated certain things. We have been in situations where we contradicted ourselves because we didn't practice what we preached. Most importantly we all sin and fall short of the glory of God. Still in all, you must play the game in order to win at it. Even in playing the game, there are still lines that shouldn't be crossed, and some words left unspoken.

Our definition of keeping it real, is not the real definition. Truth be told, none of us are really keeping it real. We say we are keeping it real because it's a classic cliché. Therefore, we really don't know the difference. In my own life, *I've learned that keeping it real means knowing who and what you are, who and what to follow, and where you desire to be internally and spiritually.*

Let's look at this from a societal standpoint. We live in a world that is big on reality television. Is a reality show really depicting what is going on in the characters life? Is the reality star being defined by a mirage that is being created to entertain others at their expense? They are creating fame and making money, but at the expense of what. The money and fame have nothing to do with the real person.

## What Is Really Important in Our Society?

I find it very strange, but the most important things in life, are the least talked about in our society. It's strange because you would think that anything harmful to humans, would be addressed at an urgent pace. Realistically, most of the time, it's the opposite. The things that harm and slowly destroy us are given the most attention. They are advertised, commercialized, televised, institutionalized, publicized, and marketed all the time.

We are always being enticed with advertisement about cigarettes, pornography, regular or prescription drugs, alcohol, fast food, get rich fast money schemes, credit cards, car dealership lies, and fake church ads. This is just a few, there are plenty more. Keep in mind, these are all outward body influences that will sometimes take us away from the real influential things, or the real problems at hand.

This is funny and to avoid getting frustrated and mad, you sometimes must laugh it off to keep yourself from doing something stupid or making it worse. So instead of getting angry and going off, you laugh it off, and slowly try to come up with a positive solution, that starts with facing the reality of things.

It's weird because, there are people who really know what's going on. They know the seriousness of it, yet ignore it, and act like they see or know what's going on. These are the same people who go around saying they are keeping it real.

It's sad because, you might want to help as much as you can, to expose, reveal, address, and express it, and at the same time you want to cry because, realistically, you know these things are silent killers. Again, it's not because some of us don't know, it's more because we don't care enough to change, correct, or do something about it.

We actually adopt the attitude that says I am not going to say anything even though I know right from wrong. I know not to abuse my body with drugs and alcohol. I know not to eat junk food or fast food every day, all day. I know how to express or address my sadness or pain. What they do is their business, it is not my issue or problem! This simply means that we see the problem yet choose to ignore it. This type of attitude is detrimental.

## Mental Self Inflicted Pride

Outward pride slowly, and uncontrollably destroys, pollutes, and damages our minds. It's like being set up by self, verses being set up by another person or thing. Too many of us are allowing ourselves to be subjected to mental and emotional control. Certain things are not seeable almost to a fault. It's not like you can look inside yourself and see your emotions. It's not like you can go outside of your brain and see what's on your mind or can you!

Someone might come and ask the classic question, "What's on your mind?" Do you really tell them based on what you are thinking and feeling? Inwardly or outwardly? Is this feeling directly from you, or is this feeling based on something or someone else? If it is based on outside influence, your state of mind at this point is used to doing what it is controlled or designed to do. Which is to drift away from your true inward self, to the outward self that is controlled my society. People can ask you every day, "How are you doing?"

Regardless of how you are really feeling, you will more than likely respond with the same answer. And because you might be pulling away from the real you, which is the truth within yourself, you will respond with the same routine answer. "I'm good" or "I'm okay", which of course is the false you. They are asking how you are doing because they can't see the inside of you, which is again your truth, but at this point neither can you. You can be just as lost about your truth as the person who is asking.

We have been programmed to say what we think people want to hear. You might know exactly what your issue is, but don't want to disclose it for personal reasons and you have that right. I would call this your truth being twisted into a personal lie. This could go on for quite some time and someone might pry the truth out of you eventually, which means it is now no longer a lie.

It wasn't just a lie, it became a painful lie, and that's how some of us men handle, and deal with our pain, concerning our emotions. It's a bunch of pain that at its highest level or capacity could cause even the strongest man to explode like a volcano. Painful feelings that are not addressed should never be ignored men and women! It could be a pain caused by unforgiveness, physical abuse (which we will discuss later), or losing your lady. No matter the cause, pain is still pain.

You could have been abused growing up and never received counseling. Maybe you witnessed your siblings being abused, molested, or raped. Your mind tells you that you're good, but could it be that it took an emotional toll on you that is unresolved. Sometimes we put up emotional defense codes. It would be extremely hard for a man to move forward after being emotionally damaged by a woman he confided in, who knows his secrets, cried in front of, was engaged to, and has a baby with.

If this has not been addressed externally or openly this brother would not be in a good state of mind. The investment is too deep. The heart is too emotionally attached to the woman. There must be a sense of closure. This goes back to the pride and ego thing. How much pride do you have? Of course, we are talking about the outer pride.

Are you afraid to show your pain? Do you believe that you could really move on without dealing with the pain if you were in this man's shoes? Does this man really even know how to identify his feelings and the inner-self that is connected to his emotion? These are the questions that are not processed and asked sometimes. If they are asked, they are often ignored or unaddressed. This is when self-inflicted pain takes over. His state of confusion creates a false identity that consumes him.

Let's take a closer look at the scenario. This man becomes the victim of a broken heart after losing his woman. He feels like it is not his problem or issue to address, slowly being fooled that she is the problem not him! Now of course, there are two sides to every story. In the relationship either party is subject to get hurt, but we also tend to hurt ourselves in the process. No matter how the pain was inflicted, it became a problem that needs to be solved by the man.

Therefore, it is crucial for this brother to protect his heart, because it is his heart that is or was broken! Not to say the woman wasn't affected, but this is a matter of self-preservation. Don't suppress your pain; deal with it (pain) before it deals with you.

# CHAPTER FOUR

## "Pride Hidden In Relationships"

Since this topic is on relationships, I will explain by using myself as an example. I have hurt enough women in my life alone, to understand the seriousness of pride and how it affects relationships. I now realize, what goes around comes around. You will definitely reap what you sow, especially in relationships. This is a painful fact I am still experiencing. My heart has always been to motivate, inspire, honor, appreciate, and love women, but my expressions didn't always come out the right way.

I've been hit, slapped, punched, threatened, and cursed out so many times I lost count. You may be asking, why? As I continue telling my truth, that question will soon change to, why not? With that being said, change is something we all, both men and women must experience at various points in our lives. Change can either make or break us depending on how we respond to it. Change in relationships is usually the hardest to adapt to and get over.

When we as men, hear the words "it's over" we quickly jump to defense and tend to go overboard, overexaggerate, attempt to overcompensate, or emotionally go over the cliff. Too many of us men wait until our backs are against the wall concerning our women. Then we try to concoct a fast solution to mend the situation that nine times out ten becomes a temporary one.

We are programmed to robotically fight simply because we are now used to the emotional attachment and the mental patterns. When she is fed up, we begin to realize that we really didn't express or show how we truly felt when we were supposed to. So instead of getting counseling or spiritual or emotional help, we allow our now suppressed feelings to substitute the reality or the real fundamental root that suffocates the emotion with our ego.

This particular ego cause's reality to replace the true self we were trying to display in the first place. Your false self is now led and controlled by your ego. And I am not talking about the natural ego that you were born with. I am talking about the negative or alto ego that imposes and leads the mind to believe that this is who you really are. This particular ego wants to control, be ahead of everybody, competes for no apparent reason, cares about what people thinks, strives for respect by any means necessary, and will replace your woman, I mean the truth with a lie. This ego wants you to sex your life away, drink it away, be in control, conceited, arrogant, and all the other destructive actions that will have you at its mercy!

## Managing Our Pride

Thus far you've read a lot about the outer or negative pride, however there's good pride that will allow us as men to be positive and victorious. For instance, when we show our emotional side through competing. As men we feel like it's okay to show our true feelings when it comes to a competitive victory. For example, I have witnessed several men shed tears, and cry out when they win in a competition, such as a championship game, accomplishments, some sort of team victory or maybe a personal goal. Their success causes them to get emotional in private or public.

These are considered tears of joy, peace, happiness, commitment, and togetherness. This is good pride. Where your hard work, desire, and commitment reaps a win or victory. This allows you as a man to feel good or successful. Now success is good, but many times as men we ask ourselves, "What happens if we fail?" What does failure do to us as men? Failure provides the opportunity for us to cry negatively. Instead of winning we lose, which brings me to my next point.

We as men hate to lose, because it creates a prideful emotional side that produces disappointment, frustration, and anger. There are times in life when we feel like automatic failures. We not only feel bad, but we look bad. In our inner thoughts we feel like we have failed. One of the hardest things a man can go through is failing at something he worked hard to accomplish. This can definitely make or break us.

For example, I love basketball, so I will use that as an illustration. Let's take a look at Michael Jordan. A lot of people don't realize that Michael Jordan wasn't always a winner. He wasn't always winning it all or competing at a higher level. He had to lose, which helped him to build a sense of endurance. Endurance produces perseverance, and perseverance produces character.

He had to first lose, in order to know how to win, and this built his character as a player. This continuous character growth has caused him to still be known as one of the greatest competitors in the history of sports. I genuinely believe, if Michael Jordon didn't fail the way he did at first, he would have never became a legend in the game. His competitiveness alone allowed him to be victorious in basketball, even when he lost a game. Like I said at the beginning of the book, we must allow our pride to be controlled when we lose, and in return it will be reversed, allowing us to win.

Sometimes our feelings supersede how great and awesome we should or could be. Fortunately, Jordan didn't allow his ego, or pride to hinder his success. Once again, we must learn how to control our ego or outer feelings. Don't let them get the best of you in a negative way. We ought to take pride in everything that we do, win, or lose. As men we should believe that we are courageous, competitive winners at all times.

We are winners in a lot of areas if we allow ourselves to believe it, while not being controlled by the outward focuses on society's results. Our continued focus should allow us to compete and win against our outward pride. The winning results will destroy the competition that produces humility that slowly erases and kills the outer pride.

## Pride Produces Destruction

So many of us are busy thinking about how hard life can be, instead of realizing that we make it harder on ourselves, by being programmed by society or closed up. If you read the papers, watch the news, or Google it on your computers or cell phones, you will begin to see that some disastrous things have to happen to erect change. Ladies and gentlemen- PRIDE KILLS! Pride will cause men to become destructive like a tornado taking out everything in its path.

Let's look at a man that is perceived to be mentally sane, but he tells you, not once, but twice that he is going to kill you or himself. This is not something to take lightly, but this behavior could stem from his pride being hurt or that nasty ego. This person could be a child abuser or molester in the neighborhood. We can never truly know a person's true intent.

Therefore, we can't wait until something happens and then rally up, protest, band, and write petitions after the fact. We all are to a degree guilty to reacting after, opposed to acting before. As people, we all need to wake up and understand what is real and what is fake. We need to read between the lines, watch and look out for signals and clues involving people, whether its family, friends, associates, strangers, babysitters, etc. I am not saying that we all need to watch each other like we are aliens in a foreign land or planet.

We all need to realize that everybody who says I got you, I will be there for you, I am your provider, protector, you are my brother, I am your father, you suppose to love me, let's get married, you can trust me, etc., does not mean that it's true or it will last. Be incredibly careful to not be too emotionally attached to the outward verses the inward. Longevity and experience help you to believe, fight and have faith.

However, this doesn't mean you should be naïve or that you are being disloyal. You shouldn't show unfair favoritism, or compromise your standards, or break unnecessary boundaries that you stand for within yourself.

Sometimes the emotional mind will blind you from the reality of the truth, even though it is right in front of you. There are too many prideful men and women who are too proud to get help in there respected or not respected relationships. Sometimes the pride hinders the growth or in some cases the truth. The emotional attachment of love gets in the way and turns to outward pride. You see pride sometimes supersedes the signal and signs to leave or to get help. Help for you or for your partner or help for you and your partner. We too at times are too prideful to allow people to say, "I told you so!" Which causes many of us to go through the same dangerous cycles over and over again until these issues get worse or it is too late.

We overcompensate trying to prove people wrong, not realizing that a wrong is a wrong, regardless of who is doing it or saying it. We all fall and make many mistakes that we can individually or collectively grow and learn from. I do realize that people change and for whatever reason give up or give in to all sorts of weirdness, addictions, dangerous teachings, etc. If this is the case you could be in the right situation, but with the wrong person. Or you might be with the right person and at this particular time be in an unfortunate situation. If this is the case then it is a matter of being strong, patient, and persevering through it.

Be careful to avoid emotional shortcuts that will slice you like a knife penetrating through your heart. The cutting starts off slow but will grow at a rapid pace as the mind tries to convince you that everything is okay. So now, instead of the mind operating with brain signals, it operates through emotional attachments that coincidently ignores the brain signals.

Jeremiah 17:9 says, “The heart is deceitful among all things and beyond cure, who can understand it.” This explains how the heart begins to deceive the mind that is designed to lead you, the individual away from trouble. Instead of protecting you from the trouble, it allows you to be continuously involved with it, repeating the same cycle over and over again.

# CHAPTER FIVE

## "Pride vs. Ego"

Okay we've discussed quite a bit about a man's pride, but let's take it further and talk about the ego. I have often heard people reference a man and his ego. In those times it wasn't positive, because an ego can be viewed as being negative in a sense. Just how big can a man's ego be? Can ego affect him in the same manner that pride can? The answer is "yes" it definitely can and eventually it will. Pride and ego most of the time go hand and hand. Pride can have both a negative and positive effect.

A man's ego in this term is more about himself in a conceited or arrogant way. Pride is not open and aware like the ego. With pride, most of the time we, especially men, can hide it. But with the ego it can come full circle like a 3d movie, coming right at you. Once again, you can spot a man's ego from a block away, as opposed to pride, which at times you can hide it, or allow it to be hidden for a period of time. In other words, one is very visible, where the other could be hard to see. Pride can be right in front of you without you even noticing it.

Now, as men we all have our respected egos. Some of our egos are bigger than others. This causes us to become confused on which one to follow, act on, or trust. At times it can become a see-saw battle between the two. Unfortunately, when the confusion is consistent, it does something to our minds. It basically takes over to the point of us possibly losing or being blind to its power. So instead of us controlling the two, we allow them to get out of control, and control us.

One day, we might be led by our big ego, then another day pride will attempt to take the lead. You might still be wondering how they are similar or even be in denial of the power they possess. That's okay and I understand. I've been there myself a time or two. If you were to look in the dictionary, I guarantee you the definitions may be worded differently, but are very much the same. If you look in certain dictionaries you will find the word ego and pride, in the same sentence. Pride and ego both stem from a feeling. Pride is a thought, and so is the ego.

Most of the time a man's ego, needs something to allow or create its identity for recognition. For example, he might define his ego based on people, places, or things. The things might consist of a house, a car, fame, clothes, women, etc. A man might feed his ego by wearing name brand clothes which play into his appearance. Without the clothes, his ego might be low, causing embarrassment or low self-esteem. This is when pride steps in and takes over. His embarrassment is based on a feeling, not actual truth. This may cause the man to become prideful with a negative attitude.

Instead of the man understanding the root of his ego and his emotions, he ignores them, and will more than likely wait to obtain those things that he feels will boost his ego. Let's take a closer look at the root of these emotions that the man is not willing to understand. The root is outer expression verses inner. Based on his ego, he has failed to acknowledge the fact that he needs material objects to feel valued and important.

The ego gets excited and finds fulfillment in material possessions, financial status, titles, women, etc. While the ego is being inflated, pride becomes emotionally attached to the same outer fulfillment. So instead of you being recognized by who you really are, you allow yourself in your mind to be recognized based on the outer self without realizing it. This is when the feeling turns or manifest into a pattern, or the way of life for your pride, and the ego. Both manifest from a feeling that comes from your mind, the two are actually drawn from that one place. Our mind and motions work together.

A man's ego could also be compared to a man working out at the gym. The purpose of the gym is to get muscles, which lead to more attention, self-gratification, or simply to boost or lift himself up. My question is this, "Are we building up our egos, or are we building ourselves up for success?" This is a question to truly ponder within yourself. As men we must be careful to recognize and understand what we are feeding. When the ego is fully fed, it will allow you to feel full. Full of yourself that is!

When someone's stuffed, after eating, and they continue to eat, most likely they will throw up. This means, all the food that was eaten or in this case used to boost the ego, was wasted. Another thing to be mindful of is confusing ego with confidence. Real pure, true confidence lies deep within the soul. This type of confidence is respected because it's not self-focused or harmful. It understands that self-motivation is needed to accomplish a particular or specific goal. Whereas the ego is mostly focused on itself and no one else. It doesn't care what its up against, but totally relies on its past accomplishments.

Hopefully, you understand or realize the difference because understanding is a part of changing the problem. If you don't understand what the problem is, then it's absolutely nothing to change. This brings me to my next point. As men we are sometimes beaten up inside. Some of us are aware, and some of us are not. For the ones that are aware, we sometimes hide it. For those of us who will show it, it might be in the form of competition.

For example, if somebody poses a challenge to us, we are ready to compete. Why, because most men like to win in any and every competition. So we will do everything to make ourselves look good, for that respective victory. Some of us will do anything to win even if it compromises who we really are, or to what is really visible. A man like this feels like, if he loses, it will tear his ego apart. And if a man feels like his whole life should revolve around his ego, then he is lost, confused, brain washed, and misled to a degree.

When I say misled in this particular passage, I'm talking about being misled by the streets or society. It's basically being led to believe something about us as men that is wrong. But because we have believed it for so long, it's hard to see the truth or even to understand what the truth is. As men, we do not want to allow our egos to make us believe that we have failed. Yes, it's that big "F" word, *failure*! As men we need to understand that sometimes failing at something is a good thing. It could be good because whatever you might have failed at, the next time you will have the capacity to be prepared and to come harder and stronger.

Failure has the potential to produce both perseverance and endurance. You might have lost the competition, but what about the lesson learned. What about the nuggets obtained that can carry you into your future? You might be labeled as a loser, because in most competitions there can only be one winner but winning is more mental than physical.

Yet, many of us still refuse to understand or grasp this concept. Instead, we want to win at everything, not realizing if we did, there would be no room for growth. When we arrive at a place of knowing it all and having achieved it all that's when it's time to go home to God. Every day is a new day to grow, learn and challenge yourself as a man to be greater than the day before. You might ask, to grow in what?

If you don't feed the body with the right foods and ingredients for a long period of time, what will eventually happen? The body will get used to the bad nutriments and probably be confused enough not to fight them off. And when the good foods come along, because it's used to the bad, it might reject the good.

Which will allow the body not to grow correctly, and according to the person, it might self-destruct slowly, but surely. The same thing happens to the heart and mind when it's not properly growing in good company. It might not understand what true failures or shortcomings really are. Instead of feeding off of wasted energy for the ego, it feeds into it. It slowly gets schooled or corrupted by negative energy.

# CHAPTER SIX

## "Unresolved Pain"

Most men hide pain for two reasons. One reason is not knowing how to deal with it without feeling weak, silly, stupid, or soft. Therefore, we intentionally do things to feel strong, smart, hard, and/or to look good, which again is nothing but outward pride. We basically without realizing it ***hide what we feel, to look real***. The second reason we hide is because we might be afraid of it, depending on what type of pain it is. More than likely we are trying to avoid hurting someone, so we deceive the pain, which makes it worse.

Pain is not supposed to be unaddressed. Pain is not supposed to settle on the inside of us. If and when it happens it is supposed to go through a process. This process should start with the infraction and end with healing. Key word is *should*. When we try to hide or ignore pain it will eventually try to force itself out at a full rate of speed, which has the potential to do great damage to all involved.

This is unfortunately how patterns and labels are formed for the MAN! This is the very reason why so many women say the following...

*"Once a cheater, always a cheater!"*

*"All men are dogs!"*

*"Men don't listen!"*

*"Men think with their penis!"*

*"I'm going to start dating women!"*

These particular women, if it applies, put up defense codes! This isn't good because both the male and the female are interacting with the same defense mechanisms. Neither party is willing to expose their hearts unless he or she is convinced to reveal the code! These codes might consist of bitterness, anger, unforgiveness, the scary code of depression and/or suppression. These defense codes have the potential to become a strong hold that is unbreakable naturally.

Addictions and cycles are now the basic reality for this group of people. They may not realize it, but they begin feeding off each other's dysfunctions. I truly feel we as a culture or society have it all backwards. This opinion is based on our different patterns, lifestyles, or sayings. For example, I personally don't like when people say, "What I don't know, or what I don't see, can't and won't hurt me." There goes the defense code again. These statements make we wonder, if these people really know what they are speaking into the atmosphere.

Now granted, I understand their logic. Most people who make that statement are in relationships, and they have been hurt, or don't want to be hurt, so they are blindly trying to protect themselves from any future hurt. However, some exposure to pain is good. It allows you to grow once you overcome it, with the intent of eventually learning from it. Think about it for a minute. Have you ever tried to hide or prevent something, but it managed to happen anyway? Just think if you would have faced it head on, the pain from the blow might not hurt as bad and the pain not last as long.

Trying to protect yourself from emotional pain tends to create more pain based on how you respond to it. Everything happens for a reason. The problem is our desire to speed up time. As if we have the power to create it. Only God has the power to control time. We should be willing to take the time to process the reason or lesson behind the pain, but many times we don't. We interfere with the process of healing by leaning to our own understanding and this gets us in major trouble.

The Bible states, "That pain and suffering is a reality, that's needed for everyone." We as men must be willing to understand the pain enough to see it clear on all levels. There are times that pain is visible, without us really noticing it. We see pain all day, every day, week after week, month after month, 365 days of the year. Be it on television, hearing about it on the radio, seeing it right in front of us, or experiencing it on our own. Pain is talked about, acted out, performed, premeditated, rehearsed, provoked, copied, endorsed, promoted, and built up! The sad but true thing is the silent pain that is built up, is the pain that hurts the most!

This pain, so to speak, comes out of nowhere, so we think! This is how suppression is formed. A state of shock becomes a form of denial. Substitutions began to create a false sense of solutions, if the mind (pain), sends the message to the body that it is okay. Now the pain sits inside the man for an extended period of time allowing him to believe he is good. If this applies, certain reactions are no longer necessary for this man, causing him to believe that no one or nothing bothers him. So now, the things that are actually bothering him, are internally hidden or causing physical pain to the body.

However, pain is not the actual makeup of the man. This is simply a part of the man that needs to be released, dealt with, and not denied. When we fail to properly do this, we create a false version of ourselves that is carrying real pain. So, does this mean that pain is unavoidable? In some aspects that would be a strong, yes! In other aspects no. I say no because there are times that pain has nothing to do with us (men) inwardly or individually. Still in all, it is still what it is- PAIN!!! Pain can come in many forms such as people, friends, family members, co-workers, husbands, wives, children, past experiences, or someone else's failures. This can even happen at times when we are minding our own business.

Pain interrupts our comfort zones, and it doesn't play fair. The sad thing is, it doesn't have rules, nor does it have a schedule. It will and can appear when you least expect it. Pain if it doesn't get you the first time, will circle back around to catch you again. There are those men who will suppress the pain, acting like it was never there, or they are over it, but it never left. Pain doesn't just go away on its own. For many of us it is a matter of trying to run from it, knowing we don't have the emotional legs that are strong enough to neither run nor stand on. No offense to people who can't walk. But I know you readers understand the important point!

I'm sure you remember those classic, famous karate movies, where there were two well trained fighters fighting at the end. Before the movie is over, we already know that one is going to kill the other. In this competitive interaction the two fighters are thinking the same thing. Either I take him out, or he will take me out. This further explains the point of this chapter. When pain enters your life, the intent is to kill, steal and destroy. Like the fighters you have to determine if you are going to defeat the pain, or the pain defeat you. Substituting the pain will never work. Hiding the pain is only temporary and will eventually make itself known.

Unlike the Kung Fu fighters who express their skills, by fighting to survive, there are times when we as men choose not to fight. We do this for two reasons in particular. One reason is we feel like we are going to lose the fight, so we avoid the showdown. The second reason is, not knowing how to fight. I am not talking about physical fighting. I am talking about fighting to manage our emotions. Now if we feel like we are going to lose, then it's because of a hidden reason, which is the root that is most of the time causing us to be in pain in the first place. We hide the pain within ourselves by not exposing and expressing it. This is called self-inflicted pain. Pain we inflict upon ourselves without realizing it.

We discussed the outer pride, which slowly kills a man, which further emphasizes the fact that the most important things are the ones that are unseen. Well, it's not like you can see pride, the way you can see anger and pain. You can look into a man's eyes and see his pain. But can you look into his eyes and see that his pride is painfully killing him? Of course not! The only way you might see it, is by what he says, or how he talks.

Another way you might detect it, is by the way he acts. Or if you knew him for a long time, you might realize he is being fake, or phony, because he doesn't want to reveal the truth.

He would rather live a lie, than to be exposed. Not realizing that eventually the lie will expose him on every level when it's fully grown and ready to give birth to death. I don't mean a physical death, but an emotional death that affects every area of a man's life. I believe pride has caused many men to settle and miss out, compromise, and hide, self-inflict and damage, ignore reality, and constantly live in denial. As a result, talents and purpose go unnoticed, overlooked, replaced, ignored, or disrespected.

Once again, if this applies, the defense code combined with the added pain and frustration becomes a bunch of red flags. Red flags that appear to be false alarms to those who know us. For some of us, instead of reacting to a fire or important predicament, we ignore the alarm while thinking the solution is to keep pressing the off button. Now this false alarm, becomes the false you that replaces the real you, inflicting more pain on the inner man and the physical body. And we all know when pain enters the human body, male or female, it cannot dwell for long.

The longer the pain dwells in the body the weaker the body or the person becomes! Hopefully, respectfully, and gracefully, my goal is not to expose a man's weakness. Believe you me, it's the opposite. I'm a man myself, but my goal is to expose a man's strength (real men cry), that has been hidden for decades and even centuries.

As I get older, I am continuously becoming more aware of who I am inside and out. I am still currently learning a lot about me. My goal is to know myself more today than I did yesterday. And God willing, I will know myself more tomorrow than I do today. I am slowly beginning to realize that having this mindset is good for my mind, heart, soul, and body. My soul needs to be reminded daily of what's going on inside of me, like a newspaper, or the daily news.

# CHAPTER SEVEN

## "A Lethal Hidden Pain"

Now before I begin, I would like to first give my condolences to the souls of men and women who lost their battle with pain to suicide and pray for their families. My reason for writing about such a touchy subject is to bring awareness and to advocate for people to get help for the hidden emotional trauma that constantly knocks at the door or their soul.

The strange thing is this, the emotion or feeling is not really hidden, because there is a continuous reminder that it never left. Any type of negative feeling you have, will continue to resurface unless you deal with it or release it. It's almost like putting a band aid on a flesh wound and expecting it to heal. Not only will the wound not heal, but it will also create a new scab and more damage. How many times have you read in the papers or seen on television that someone committed suicide by jumping off a roof, or maybe overdosing on pills? How many times have you heard people say, "I didn't see any signs or signals of suicide?"

To be honest, they are probably right, because the signs we are taught to look for, are sometimes not the obvious ones. Realistically we all become used to what we see and experience every day. So, to us these alarming signs become normal. In one way or another we tend to feed off one another. We as people have to be willing to be in each other lives more.

If your soul does not fellowship consistently, it begins to wander and drift out of its state of pure consciousness. Like Adam and Eve who wondered and drifted away from what was good inwardly or spiritually speaking, and as a result got booted out of the garden. Another example is that of a young child who wonders away. During their time of wondering, they tend to get into a lot of trouble and by time you find them the damage is already done.

Then you might have that individual who is always around people, but never says anything to anyone unless he is spoken to. You, I, or we all might think that this person is fine because he is always around people. Yet, little did we know that he wanted to talk, but was in so much pain that he couldn't, or it was hard to get it out. All those feelings and emotions were trapped and bottled up inside of him, to the point they were unbearable. As a result, he self-destructed which led to an emotional release that could only be solved through death.

Which brings me to my next point. Feelings that are not addressed can be fatal. I can boldly say that too many of us (men and women) are emotionally committing suicide. We allow these feelings to control us rather than controlling them! At this point in the book, you might feel a little beaten up, wounded, or scarred, if you are a man. If that is how you feel, GOOD! This means you are FEELING and my purpose for writing this book is being fulfilled. If you remain focused and inspired, I guarantee it will all pay off in the end. You will better understand why you needed to read this book and why I needed to write it. We are both gaining something greater.

I must make this declaration - *Men will continue to strategize, plan and focus, regardless of the past, present, or current circumstances or situations!*

All men, I repeat, all men need to have vision, dreams, plans, and goals! Every man needs encouragement regardless of who he is, what level he's on, how much money he has, how popular he is or is becoming, how many people look up to or follow him, how many times he blew it, failed, or lost. All men desire to be respected whether he wins or loses, or his plans fail or succeed. Now the level of respect, or how much respect he gets causes a man to form a sense of importance or ego. If he wins, the ego begins to manifest into to what you read about earlier (PRIDE). This respected ego or pride can do two things to the individual (man).

This egotistical pride is the form of the ego searching for honor or respect! These two things are now respected attributes or characteristics that can sometimes make or break us men. Break us out of the formed ego or make us into strong men of inner pride. Once again, this inner pride is the pride that will make us great established achievers that deserves honor. Being honored is one of the greatest feelings I believe as men we need to go after and seek. This is nothing more than going after the desires of our hearts. Now of course when we go after the respected desires of our hearts, sometimes frustration, a lack of patience, jealousy, people hating on our dreams, not believing in us, lack of support, and all sorts of distractions begin to take place.

This is a good thing though, only of course if we stay focused on the goal at hand. A vision must be thought out and processed first. Second, it must be tested on many levels. Some of these tested levels are all the above topics so far that you have read in this book. I call these levels, the levels of spirits! These different spirits are tested respectfully and repeatedly. These levels once again, will test us to the max! These levels look us face to face, deal with us issue to issue, will mold, and shape our character trial after trial, tribulation after tribulation, time after time.

When it's all said, and done, as far as the circumstances and predicaments we overcome, this spirit will become a reality to our daily lives that will seem so real to the point where it will ask us questions to determine whether we have arrived. Of course, you the reader are asking "arrived from what." The question is this, "Did everything go as planned?" The vision that we set forth in our minds to go forward, has it been accomplished? Do we feel like we have succeeded? Are we in the right frame of mind as far as our emotions or feelings? Unfortunately, many men leave these questions unanswered.

We overlook or ignore the actual issues that allow us to question the problems instead of looking to solve them! Instead of us looking within ourselves to define the reason, we sometimes look outside of ourselves and look at society's solutions and reasons. Television ads, radio program shows, and endorsements become some of our focus to find the reasons why our goals and dreams look unrealistic. Here come the questions again, this time coming from all the people who we told our dreams and visions too. They are the ones now asking us, with a puzzled look on their face, "What happened to the publishing company you were supposed to open? What happened to the business you were supposed to start? Where is the woman you said you were going to marry? Where is the big house you were going to have with the five bedrooms and pool in the back yard?

While these annoying, frustrating, mind consuming questions are being asked, we at the same time are asking ourselves word for word, the same exact questions. *Where did we go wrong?* What stopped us from achieving or accomplishing the goals that we set at the beginning of the year? What got in the way, or what distracted us from the well thought out plan that was supposed to take place months ago?

Now we can respectfully go back to the spirits that I mentioned in the beginning of the chapter. In our day to day life, from the time of birth until now, we all go through different forms, growth, maturity levels, places and experiences that are designed to teach us how to live and succeed in life. Now, while we go through these different levels of life, we also continue to deal with adversity, trials, tribulations, and different energy levels of people. We begin to develop character, emotion, attitudes, dignity, ego, and many more important attributes that will help us to understand what went wrong.

The unfortunate thing at times, is we men, don't wait patiently for the process of the question to manifest an answer. We become bitter, defensive, finger pointing, and frustrated while trying to answer the question by ourselves, without having any real resources as to why we are not at the level we feel we should be. This takes us back to the spiritual levels! Thinking of a master plan is not the problem. Realizing that it will take everything you have to accomplish it is. There is nothing wrong with making millions, wanting to comfortably provide for your family, or creating something that society will benefit from. Just know that it might take longer than expected.

Yes, this doesn't fit within our perfect plan or appeases those people questioning you, laughing at you, mocking you, gossiping about you, fronting on you, or betraying you, family included. These different people slowly but surely become the first step away from our actual spirit! These people become the excuses and the blame for our shortcomings, or our failures; of course, in our minds. If we don't blame these people, we take it out on them, making them the reason or the target of the pain that resides in our hearts.

Sometimes this feeling of failure or shortcomings become a spirit. The amount of pain will determine the consequences. Unfortunately, the focus is shifted on people, places, and things, such as material achievements, and accomplishments like houses, cars, money, fame, popularity, ego boost, and a feeling of importance! Keep in mind, I am not talking about all men, but the majority not the minority. The continued different levels of pain become the levels of the spirit in you (man), and the spirits of people. The argument or the question started out innocent. Why am I failing? Why haven't my blessing come forward yet? Why is he or she being blessed when I did the same thing, or more way before them?

Do you see the development? You can see the blame-shifting or finger pointing spirit, along with a comparison or envious spirit. Then there is an impatient spirit developing to the point of having no direction or focus on the individual itself, even though he is asking the question. Sometimes the problem is perseverance and faith haven't been established yet. This could be the very reason why nothing has happened or manifested. The frustration, the lack of patience, the blame shifting, the questioning of God, is the new focus with no answer or solution. So, the more the questioning with no answer, the more the spirit level is emerging to its full compacity, where it will soon explode like a volcano waiting to erupt!

Unfortunately, the eruption becomes, pain on top of pain, where we hear the famous sayings,

*"Bad company corrupts good character!"*

*"Misery loves company!"*

*"The blind can't lead the blind!"*

*"What does light have to do with darkness?"*

Some of you are probably asking, "What is the point?" Well, I'm glad you asked. The point is this, the same way we have goals and plans for ourselves and our family, God and the devil does to! This is why talking about spirits is relevant. If you read your bible and believe what you read, you will fully understand the passage of scripture that talks about the battle is beyond what we can see, know, hear, or feel. We wrestle not against flesh and blood, but principalities and spiritual wickedness in high places. If we are not careful as men, we can develop a me, myself, and I syndrome. Which means we are not focusing on the things of God that bring clarity and wholeness, we are focusing on the flesh which reaps destruction.

Focusing on self has caused a lot of men to fall and fail at accomplishing their goals. Me, I or my; is not what the true spirit of God would like for us to understand or believe. This selfish mentality comes after the frustration, the anger, and the ego get involved. This is when the soul is introduced to the evil one, Lucifer, Satan, or the devil! The principalities or spirits that enter or that is trying to enter take us away from who we are, where we are trying to get to, or detour us away from our purpose, especially concerning our emotions! Any type of negative emotional feeling is not from God.

That particular feeling if it's not addressed is not the target, the goal, or the plan to try to get the man or men to be successful. This man is thrown off, and not only is he thrown off his focus and course; but he has a spirit on his back trying to permanently destroy his vision, dreams, and goals. This is the war that we go through inside our minds when we are not where we feel we need to be. Unfortunate things begin to happen to some of us that are fatal and life changing; causing us to play catch-up in life. Sadly, jail or prison becomes a normality that causes a lot of us to have too much time taken away from us. This allows us to play the pity party with our feelings.

And it's something about the word FEELINGS; that scares most of us men without us even realizing it.

With that being said, my goal and vision on writing this book, is to help us men to correctly release our emotional state, to achieve our dreams and goals, to encourage ONE ANOTHER, to stay real and remain focused. Some of us are put in situations that we have no choice but to pay attention and be focused on a plan or goal. That plan or goal is to be released from our pain and suffering. If it doesn't affect us as far as suffering then some of us fool ourselves into thinking that just because it is not us fighting and praying to be released from those demons, or mental and emotional, or even physical issues; we are good?

Now that selfish spirit is jumping from one person to the next. So, all these men who believe they are good because they are not going through poverty, prison, substance abuse, etc. are silently being affected sometimes worse than all of the above. And you might ask why, or how? Reason being is, hidden pain is the WORSE! The worst attack is when the persons guards are down, not allowing him to defend himself. At least when these KINGS and WARRIORS go to prison; they know exactly what their vision, dreams and goals are and that is "TO GET THE HELL OUT!"

These men continuously fight to focus on their character which allows them to overcome the shortcomings, or the upcoming struggles of life after prison. And granted, we all make mistakes, we are all human beings that are not made to be perfect. A lot of men make mistakes when it comes to jail or prison. Some of us are simply at the wrong place at the wrong time. Some have too much idle time and waste it on foolishness that leads to foolish things with the result being behind bars.

Not all, but some of us try our hardest to feed our families, get out of the ghetto, or get that 9-5 job, only to get laid off. This leads to selling drugs, stealing, or robbing which land you in jail. All of this creates a trained spirit of ANGER! Add anger to a frustrated and irritated heart, attached to a five year prison term, and coming home to his woman or excuse me; somebody else's woman now. This creates the spirit of revenge!! The emotional pain in his body that is attached to his spirit is holding on because of his pride and joy, his baby girl or daughter.

She is the sole reason why he has not taken anybody's life. He wants to enjoy his life with his daughter. Now and only now is he beginning to see the big picture. This powerful, smart, and intelligent man is starting to see light at the end of the tunnel. He has been introduced to the spirit of God. The prison time taught him how to persevere, endure, be patient, trust the process, and most of all depend on and pray to God. Men, stay focused, have faith, and believe in yourself, despite how bad it looks, those agonizing spirits inside of your family's bloodline, the spirit of jealousy that was in your so called best friend's heart, or the envious spirit that was floating around your whole community.

Always remember, until somebody breaks the spiritual strongholds of poverty, pain, anger, frustration, and the likes they will continue to plague you and future generations. Has it ever crossed your mind that you might be the bloodline breaker? You, yes YOU, just might be the one ordained by God to bring change to your family. It doesn't matter how you start, what matters is how you finish!

For all the men who are in prison hoping and praying for a second, third or tenth chance, just stay humbled and focused. Don't allow prison to destroy you, reverse the curse, and destroy it, by expressing and releasing true inner freedom within yourself. Don't continue to be in denial and stop denying your heart the opportunity to heal and become free. There are many men, such as myself who had their freedom taken away as little boys. I have never experienced hard prison time, but unfortunately, I allowed myself to become mentally and emotionally institutionalized.

# CHAPTER EIGHT

## "Humility Destroys Pride"

There are several reasons why we should avoid being controlled by pride. Remember, the outer pride is the ego mixed with flesh, and it is designed to focus on any and everything that is not of you! Even though your flesh is a part of your body, and your ego is a part of your mind, both of these parts are not meant to lead you. Instead, these different parts or negative spirits will more than likely get us into a lot of trouble. The more we chase after temporary fulfillments, the more they fool us into believing that we actually benefit from having them.

On the other hand, we would greatly benefit from learning patience, which is a vital part of obtaining success. As men, we should never base success on the external. We should never be fooled into thinking that we need to be more successful than the next man. Once we start competing at a high level trying to prove we are better than the next man, a humbling experience will take place. 2 Corinthians 10:12 says, "We do not dare to classify or compare ourselves with some who commend themselves. When they measure themselves by themselves and compare themselves with themselves, they are not wise."

Hopefully, you can grasp Gods view of this very point! You have a choice of being humbled by life or humbled by God. God is the only one who can truly judge and commend us at the same time, without speaking about anyone else. Getting to know our inner man, what we want, and why we exist, allows us to focus on us! This means we are focusing on self as the individual without including anyone else. God gives us all free will to do this important inner search. There are times when this creates a problem. There are times when we choose to use this choice of freedom to chastise, hate on, and be envious of, jealous, scheme against, or just flat out try our hardest to stop our brothers from reaching a potential or goal that is designed for us to obtain or reach together.

Nowadays, we call it stepping on somebodies' toes. This becomes a cycle that is hard to break, simply because, most men step into war mode trying to defend and protect what is his. So instead of us fighting the evil spirit that is trying to invade our hearts and minds; we do the opposite. We feed into it by believing that we have to compete and be our own keeper, instead of our brother's keeper. This becomes a question that we will continuously have to answer based on the trials and tribulations to come.

Therefore, we must be willing to ask ourselves some choice questions that must be answered, based on how we treat one another when trouble or conflict comes.

*Am I humble or prideful?*

*Am I ready, willing, and able to sacrifice something that I want or desire to make a way for someone else?*

I'm sure talking about sacrificing self for the sake of others sounds ridiculously scary. Are we willing to finish last, to give someone else the opportunity to finish first? For every man that is full of outward pride, this is a test question that will help release the spirit of selfishness caused by pride if you are willing to work diligently at it. Like I said earlier, I believe we were put here on this earth to make each other better, not just to achieve success by ourselves. If that were the case, wouldn't we be here by ourselves?

This leads me to my next point. How can we choose good inner pride over bad outer pride, while being there for one another? The answer is *to become or remain humble.* Through all of the competition and challenges life has to offer, I will ask the question again. How are we going to sacrifice ourselves to make each other better and still win and be victorious?

I'm going to use Jesus Christ, who to me, was and is the greatest example of all time. Jesus was very compassionate, sacrificial, merciful, always humble, and very obedient. He is the proven son of God, who was intelligent, knew the word of God, was the word of God, raised people from the dead, healed the sick, forgave sins even before He went to the cross, and didn't judge a single person! He was God fearing, loving, and caring towards everyone.

But unfortunately, He was still flogged, humiliated, beaten beyond recognition, wrongfully accused and crucified to death. You just read how some men fall into a spirit of competition to prove that they are better than the next man. Well, I would like to pose a question to you as the reader.

*WHO can truly compare themselves to Jesus?*

*Who could persevere and go through such a thing, and still remain focused on the goal at hand?*

*Which one of you, including myself, could be betrayed and left for dead by people you taught, broke bread with, perform miracles on and still love them to DEATH?*

I do mean literally to DEATH! If you haven't seen "The Passion of The Christ" produced by Mel Gibson, I would highly recommend watching it to get a clearer understanding of who Jesus was and how He humbled himself to the point of death on the cross. Before He went to the cross to die for humanity, Matthew 25:35, describes how Jesus asked for another way. It shows how He wanted the same support He had given many before this disastrous event. It explains how He foreknew that He would be betrayed by the people. But Jesus also knew that He had a choice. He had the same free will that God gives to us all.

Now with all that being said, imagine how you would feel? Having the foreknowledge of getting beat beyond recognition, knowing that your skin would be ripped off your physical body, knowing that you would be laughed at, ridiculed, mocked, spit on, and dragged and forced to carry your own cross, only to hang from it for hours before eventually taking your last breath. Imagine being there. Imagine taking His place. Imagine your level of pride, your emotions, your mindset, or your thoughts?

If we look at Jesus praying in the garden, He said, "Father if it by Thy will, take this cup from me, if not my will, let thy will be done." The scripture tells us that He was praying this prayer while sweating blood. This means that Jesus was having an emotional moment, based on a negative life changing circumstance and situation. He knew His purpose for coming into the earth, which means His spirit was willing, but when the time got close, His flesh got weak. Jesus was in his feelings! Jesus had emotions just like us. He cried outwardly, to God not wanting to be crucified, and then prayed inwardly for us to be forgiven of all of our sins.

He basically compromised His relationship with God in heaven, came down to earth, and sacrificed His life to save ours. Do you better comprehend the difference between inner and outer pride? Jesus' example of inner and outer pride was absolutely brilliant! He did not choose His outer pride over His inner pride. Jesus' inner pride allowed Him to remain focused and humble in that difficult circumstance and situation.

To be clearer, His emotional side, or His outer pride could have said, "Wait a minute", I am the son of God. His ego could have said, I raised Lazarus from the dead, I turned water into wine, I walked and taught people how to have enough faith to walk on water, I healed the blind, I fed the hungry, forgave all twelve disciples." He could have rightfully and powerfully destroyed everyone, one by one, or all at once.

Had He chosen self, there is no doubt that His father God could have sent the twelve legions of angels to rescue Him instantly and destroyed the whole earth. He could have said, "I don't have to die for all humanity." His explanation could have simply been that men are the ones who sinned, not Him and He would have been rightfully justified. He could have given examples to prove His point, and said, "They are killers, murders, rapist, thieves, betrayers, corrupt, evil, ungrateful, selfish, prideful, arrogant, lost, egotistical, and hateful." His outer pride could have allowed him to rebel against God's will. Instead, He chose His inner pride that said, "Yes, I am the Son of God, His only begotten son, so I will die for man's sins, because they can and will change!"

He chose to live out the plan that His father created to save us through Him. There was no ego, no outer pride, no blame shifting, no hard feelings, no complaints, no threats, no evil intent, no casting stones, and no special treatment!! Jesus had feelings. He had humble feelings that were good. These feelings were emotionally attached to you, me, and God. Even though He didn't want to die physically, He still did it for us. Those same feelings He expressed, allows us to be victorious, because those were feelings of love towards you and me. He sacrificed His life to save ours and at the same time gave us an incredible example to follow in difficult times, especially dealing with our emotions.

As men, we are faced with life changing dilemmas every day. The question becomes...

*"What decisions are we going to make?"*

*"Which pride are we going to choose?"*

*"Are we going to allow our pride to hold us back, or are we going to choose to be humble; which in turn will allow us to be successful in this world to move us forward?"*

*"Do we believe that pride can save us, or destroy us?"*

Pride is not something, we as men should take lightly! It can lead us to prosperity, and success, or it can lead us to disaster and destruction. It doesn't matter, where we are, what issues we have, whatever the circumstances might be, or what situations we are in, we can still shine and be in control of our lives. God gives us life, it's up to us whether we are going to live it in a positive way or not. We are powerful when we apply ourselves. When we are focused, we are unstoppable!

When our backs are against the wall we are at our best. Because our best has no choice but to come out, to save, rescue, release and restore us. However, some of us need to be transformed, and restored from ourselves. We might not cry outwardly, but inwardly some of us are crying. I believe deep down on the inside; most men want to release and express their feelings; just like Jesus did. We just don't know how to release, respond, and react. Or we know how, but we are afraid, and this is when we open the door for pride to put us in an emotional penitentiary.

Our feelings are sometimes caged or locked up. Still in all, I believe it's better than being physically imprisoned. Mentally and emotionally, we have the power to free ourselves! Some of us just need to be taught how. Jesus didn't allow His feelings to dictate the truth concerning His fathers will. He reacted, released, and responded to His feelings by giving them to God! He did not give them to any negative outlets, distractions, substitutions, or attempt to hide or suppress them. We as men need to be real with our feelings and stop pretending that we have them under control.

The truth of the matter is we were all born with them from the very beginning of our infant lives. Emotions are going to be with us to the day we die! When we foolishly try to hide and pretend that they don't exist we put ourselves in instant danger! I personally respect any man who does not allow their feelings to get the best of him.

For the men who know how to release, respond, and react to their feelings when needed, I want to encourage you to release yourself. Don't wait until you are cornered. Don't wait until you are chained and emotionally imprisoned to yourself. You can determine how long you are going to be locked up. You don't need a judge, a church, religion, the government, or society to determine the length of your time behind your emotional or unspiritual bars. You determine how long you are in the emotionless system that you created. Like I said before, I'm not talking about all men. I am well aware that some men are in touch with their mental, emotional, and spiritual feelings.

If you are, I commend you. May you continue on this path and prosper. I would like to take this opportunity to ask you men to educate your fellow men in and around your circle and teach them how to get in touch with who they are. Allow them to see that it's okay to express their emotions, in a positive way. Now, I'm sure you've heard of the famous saying, "Don't judge a book by its cover, read what's inside." Well, it's the same thing concerning a powerful man that may have become lost along the way. Don't count the author out just yet! Read the whole book. The ending might be exactly what you need to empower you to change.

With all due respect, I am not trying to force or prove Jesus to anyone. I only used Jesus as an example because whether you believe in Him or not, we all have to agree that He was the greatest example of a man that was humble and loving. These two attributes and characteristics are the main ingredients that we need to have in order for us to manage our emotions and feelings.

# CHAPTER NINE

## "The Three R's"

### Release, Respond, and React

My mother passed on February 2, 2006 and that was the worst day of my life. I truly didn't know how I was going to handle it. I had no idea how I would react, respond, or release the thoughts, emotions, and pain out of my heart due to her passing. I personally think I trained myself to believe that God would grant me a particular wish. Growing up as a child, I always prayed to God for my mother and father to pass on after me.

I know it sounds weird, but I really believed that I wasn't going to be able to handle it, so I prayed to God day after day that I would pass first. I'm sure some of you can relate. I realize now that one part of me didn't really want this and the other part did. The part that wanted me to pass first was the selfish, spoiled little boy in me, who was afraid to think about facing life without them.

Then there is the other side of me that realized people are going to pass first or last and this was and is beyond my control. I really wanted to enjoy life for as long as I could. So, as I got older, you better believe, I stopped requesting that particular prayer. After my mother's passing, I learned a valuable lesson as a man with a bunch of emotions, questions, requests, and prayers. I learned that in life you have to learn how to listen and face the music (so to speak). The challenges we face are valuable lessons to learn. Now it's up to you if you choose to face it, look up to it, or respect it and learn. Regardless, just please make sure you do the three R's, that is, *Release, Respond, and React.*

Keep in mind, before you release, respond, and react, you first have to identify your feelings. You have to ask yourself, *"What is the root of what I am feeling?"*
*"Where is this feeling coming from?"*
*"Is it negative or is it positive?"*

The second thing is, you must think of a healthy way to express it, especially if it's negative, such as the feeling of anger. This once again, goes back to knowing who you are and what allows you to be who you are? Too many times, we (men), deal with our feelings and emotions the same. Because we see the pattern time and time again of putting on glasses, drinking liquor, getting high, gambling, and going away for a short or long period of time after a love one dies. We think this is dealing with our pain that becomes EMOTIONAL!

The glasses or shades, represents us hiding our tears, not just from people, but hiding these release protectors from ourselves. The mind is a super powerful reader! Even though the physicality of your body is supposed to connect with your mind and its body movements, the negative spirit of anger will train your mind to believe you are not even crying, even though tears are streaming down your face! How many times have you sworn that you weren't tired and believed that you could check out a late movie, even though you yawned and actually dosed off on the way there as the driver?

As soon as the movie credits came on you went to sleep like a baby playing in his crib all day. When you finally woke up, the ending credits are rolling down the screen! Our minds can play tricks on us, while our bodies still perform as they should! Releasing and recognizing these feelings before they become emotions are the key to moving forward in a healthy manner. The body is most of the time willing; but the mind has to play catch up! When your mind is emotionally connected to a systematic way of responding to a particular discomfort, it becomes incredibly hard to break this cycle unless it is processed and released correctly!

Released patterns are sometimes unrecognized to the mind, simply because of a MINDSET. The mind is set to reject another way, which is the right or the positive way! Once again, this is how addictions are formed. This is how pattern cycles are formed! This is how strongholds and diseases are formed! This is how negative spirits come into the soul! This is the very reason why ulcers, high blood pressure, anxiety, suppression, and depression enters the body.

When my mom passed, I had to examine, and then react to this painful way I was feeling. Of course, I've felt alone or abandoned before on many levels in my life, but not to this magnitude. To be honest though, I was too young to understand how to deal with the new infested pain. It was something that no pattern or traditional teaching could teach or show me. I had to deal with this on my own. There were so many feelings and emotions going on in my mind and heart at the time that I knew I had to attack right away. One was the feeling of fear and knowing that I wouldn't see my mother again on this earth. All of those good lectures, disciplines, lessons, knowledge, and wisdom had to be stored deep inside of me. I would never hear her voice speak about them ever again.

I had to battle the fear of my father, brother and sister going through the same emotions as well. The reality was I felt alone, lost, abandoned, confused, and upset at the fact that I was going to live the rest of my life without my mother. I had to think about or ask myself, what would help me to become strong enough to overcome this painful emotional feeling before it turned to bitterness or intense anger, which turns into hatred or rage!

I began to pray for guidance and strength from God. To be honest I was tempted to rashly do the unthinkable. You are free to use your vivid imagination to figure out what I am talking about. I knew that it wouldn't be wise for me to hide my feelings by being numb to them. God's direction and guidance allowed me to release and address these feelings to my close friends. I began to be led to people who went through losing a friend or loved ones before. This was my release that further helped me to identify and examine my feelings and thoughts.

Now here comes the reaction. I slowly began to react and respond to what I was feeling, and I began to learn how the feeling became an emotion. The enact emotion allowed me to do a lot of talking, reading, and researching about life and death, sometimes enabling me to do some intense studying. Being left alone to concentrate, meditate, focus, remember, and reflect on the legacy my mother left behind.

The response and positive emotion were plaguing my heart to do something to honor her name and show people how much I loved, missed, and would always remember her. This positive reaction encouraged me to write a three page poem in dedication to her legacy. That was my reaction and my response to what I was feeling and because of it I didn't do anything negative or irresponsible that I would probably regret later. I guarantee you all, if I didn't release those feelings out of my mind and heart I would have instead destroyed and demolished everything around me.

For the first time in my entire life, I did a speech in the form of a eulogy along with Evangelist Leo Siffleit about my mother. God showed me how prayers are answered in ways that we sometimes don't expect. You see, God didn't just comfort me, He allowed me to motivate, inspire and comfort His people at the same time. He continued to show me that not only could I go on from the passing of my great mother, I would and also could help others to do the same. The funeral turned out great to the GLORY of God. So many people were touched and shocked at the same time. God began to show me how to break strongholds, cycles, and addictions without any outburst or destruction.

My point is, I got in touch with and released my true emotional pain. Thank God I did not do like some of us unfortunately do, and that is run away from, be numb to, or hide the painful feelings. Thank God I didn't turn to suicide, drugs, or try to drink my PAIN away. I truly thank God that I didn't foolishly blame or be mad at Him. I realized it was His will being done and He knows best. As time began to pass, I honestly began to even thank God for taking my mom away from this stressful, selfish, and sinful world. I began to see things clearer through this fate that we all must experience called death. I know she is no longer suffering anymore. I have faith she will be or already is in a better place.

By no means am I trying to paint this picture that I have it all together emotionally, or even spiritually. I do have the ingredients, lessons, experiences, and spiritual encounters to write this book. Everything that you are reading are things that I've had to hold myself accountable with and for. God will entertain, direct, take away, and guide your thoughts if you are alert, able and ready to give them to Him. These are thoughts that are trying to be processed and acted out by different spirits! They start out as feelings, formed into fantasies, desires, illusions, delusions, addictions, and visions; that eventually display our true emotions.

With that being said, every thought has an initial in front or behind it. The initial is trying to get you to take the tag off of and buy it. I also look at emotions like a marriage. The man and the woman have to respectfully play there part or role, before they are actually in it. First it is the courting, the puppy love, the first love stage, holding of hands, meeting each other's family, the butterflies if you will, then the proposal if you get pass the trials and tribulations that comes with dating. If you do get through the rough times, and you still want to be together then that's when the proposal comes.

Now of course, the objective, or the main idea is to allow her or him to be established as one. The one is relatable to God saying a man will leave his mother and father and be joined together with his wife. It's the same way with our emotions and feelings. They want to carry a label with us, or a tag. The tag or label is whatever the man's last name is. Wherever you go, who you interact with, who you sign with, the last name is a symbol that needs to be respected by all. I'm not saying it will, but when you see that person is taken or not available then you are supposed to move on.

Our emotions or feelings when fully formed become labels and symbols that make up our personalities and characteristics. We become married to these emotions believing that we should always be loyal and faithful to them. The issue is, sometimes we become confused to what different feelings or emotions to be faithful and loyal too. Let's keep it simple! Negative emotions are like bad habits in a marriage that form. These bad habits have to go. Sooner now, than later.

These negative bad habits that form into bad patterns, or deadly addictions has to be released. Now keep in mind, when I say released, I am not talking about broadcasting, showcasing, moping around, or uncontrollably crying hysterically or complaining about it. That is not a healthy way to deal with any feeling, especially if it's negative. I am more so talking about releasing it from your mind before it allows you to become a bitter, unhappy individual in the relationship you have with your spiritual self!

You first have to release it, before it destroys the real you. Negative emotions want to be one with your heart, mind, and spirit! Negative emotions turn into spirits that are trying to rule and control your soul. You see, negative painful feelings such as fear, anxiety, anger, sadness, hatred, losing a loved one, or jealousy when it's fully diluted in the body will cause an energy flow that will disrupt and affect the heart, the immune or nervous system, such as digestion and hormones.

This is the very reason why God tells us as humans to forgive one another. You forgive someone, or reconciling, restoring, or expressing, or even identifying the emotion is not necessarily about forgiving the person for their sake. It is forgiving that person for your own self. To keep you physically healthy and emotionally sane.

If you have some, or all of the above negative emotions in your heart and you don't react and release accordingly, your body will build up a negative emotional acid that will slowly destroy you physically and spiritually. Ignoring your emotions will not allow them to go away. You can't replace something that's not meant to be replaced. Even though an emotion is nothing but a thought or feeling, you still have to realize the affect it has on you.

This causes you to constantly relive it or rehearse it which makes it a reality to you. Instead of you releasing the emotion, you become controlled by it. This causes you to walk in unforgiveness of yourself. When I say yourself, I am not talking about the real you. I am talking about the emotional thoughts that make you think you are emotionally unstable. The same person who refuses to forgive others. If you fail to understand the root of your emotions, you are destined to become an emotional person like I was. Every friendship or relationship that I was in became an unhealthy emotional attachment that caused a lot of confusion in my life. Especially the relationships and friendships that I had with women.

# CHAPTER TEN

## "Losing Me"

When I was younger I was insecure and afraid to pursue girls that I liked or was attracted to. I created a false reaction to my true feelings. I dealt with these insecurities from the ages of 13-17, which were supposed to be my times of exploration, creativity, and experiencing puppy love. You know that first stage of love bugs that create butterflies in your stomach, and the whole I can't live without this person mentality. It wasn't until I realized that I was a talented basketball player that I began mastering my insecurities.

This is when I learned that I could master one thing yet be afraid of another. I became super confident in my ability to play basketball, but shy and still afraid when it came to young girls. So, I created a false illusion of myself without even recognizing it. I had a funny sense of humor that seemed to get people's attention. I was so funny people compared me to Eddie Murphy. Talking about pressure. I created this false illusion, and my peers were loving it, so I had to keep it up. This became my new normal. In other words, I was afraid to talk to girls when it came to dating, so I talked to them as the comedian. Instead of asking them out, I would make them laugh out of their minds.

Slowly but surely, I promoted myself and became the official class clown. Instead of doing things to make them like me, I would do silly things to make them laugh at me. When they would laugh, they would laugh so hard that tears would come out of their eyes, but little did they know, I was crying inwardly with those same tears, just for a different reason. I was basically so insecure that I was really crying out for attention. And boy, did I get it.

I would disrupt the whole entire class. I made fun of the teachers and my classmates. I did pranks like throwing things at teachers behind their backs, putting things in their seats, and making all kinds of weird sounds or noises. I would trip people in the class. I was simply a mess, to say the least.

I remember meeting my match. There was one particular teacher who was not only funnier than me, but she could fight. Yes, you read it right. I got so out of control that the teacher literally hit me. Yes, hit me, with the intention of knocking my head off. Sadly, this made me realize that I wasn't afraid of anybody. My confidence level boosted in the areas of playing basketball and fighting teachers!

I told yawl I was a MESS! So much of a mess, that I met my match and messed with the wrong teacher. Man, this teacher could fight. I won most of the fights I had with my other teachers, but not this one. Not only did she fight back, but she threw some haymakers. She was fighting like she was fighting to win. If I didn't know any better, it felt like she was fighting to win a heavy weight belt or something.

And believe it or not, to make the fight more interesting, this particular teacher didn't fight with fear; she used weapons. During one fight she hit me so hard with a ruler that it cracked over my head. The class was wilding out. Now the joke was on me, literally! It got to the point where she and I would fight every day. The more we fought, the more the class laughed.

My point is this, my hidden insecurities turned me into the class clown. This started in the second grade and pretty much lasted to the seventh. That's when I realized how much damage I was causing to myself. I began to see how focused I was on the external, versus the internal. I became a people pleaser, and we all know what happens to people who are or become people pleasers. They always end up with the short end of the stick. They get far ahead with people, but far behind with themselves.

That's exactly what happened to me. I was left behind. I had to repeat the seventh grade all over again. Not because I failed academically, but because I failed to meet the behavioral standards that were required. I was left back because of my behavior. I know you are probably thinking. What a loser! You know what; that's exactly how I felt. Like a loser! Even though I passed every class, in the end I had no class for myself. The clowning around and making people laugh got me nowhere. Deep down inside it made me feel worse than I already felt in the first place.

You talk about inner pride, I had none! You talk about outer pride, I had none! I was no longer proud of my humor; the joke was on me. Or it became me. I'm telling you with all my heart, that thing really humbled me to the core.

All my friends graduating and leaving me behind really, really hurt me. My pride and ego were crushed. It took me a long time to get over this. It caused me to develop a serious side that I didn't even know existed. Instead of playing around a lot, I became more and more serious, so serious that I would hardly play around anymore.

I allowed my insecurities and my pride to make me ashamed of who I really was. I tried to be different. I was afraid to be rejected or look bad. Instead of me being truthful to who I was, I became a fool. And believe it or not, I had to redefine who I really was. I lost ME, because I was so busy trying to be accepted by others, that I didn't accept myself. When you don't accept who you are, you don't really understand who or what you are! And what I was, is someone who was liked by many women, but was too insecure to understand what this truly meant.

As I got older women began to tell me they had a crush on me. Then and only then did I realize that my fear of rejection hindered me from enjoying the special gift of fellowship with the opposite sex. My emotions were rooted in rejection and fear. These negative emotions allowed my inner pride to blind me from seeing my worth as a man.

Now come on fellows, don’t leave me hanging. I know some of you can relate. So, to the ones who can relate, my advice to you is...

Get to know You!

Learn to love yourself FIRST!

Search for and learn the REAL you!

Be the TRUE version of yourself!

Take good PRIDE in yourself!

God made each of us exactly how He wanted us to be. Psalm 139:14 says, “And that is wonderfully made.” Accept who you are, don't try to be something that you are not. Remember, whoever does not like or accept you for who you are, guess what, it's their lost, and soon to be somebody else's gain. If you are a teenager, be careful about trying to fit in. As long as you can fit into your clothes, then you are good! Create and establish your own identity.

## My Personal Pain

We are about to discuss pain that was inflicted on innocent people, that they now must find a way to release. When people are abused, especially young girls and boys, they find themselves in a state of denial. Some develop a I don’t care attitude or it’s my fault syndrome. These victims will sometimes shift the blame off the violator and subconsciously begin to hurt people who were not responsible for their pain or abuse. They live a life filled with condemnation. I am forever frustrated and angry that most of these individuals are emotionally and mentally destroyed.

Sad to say, they become victims to themselves. With all that being said, I am eternally grateful, that I didn’t become a statistic. I didn’t become the person that was violated but took my pain out on everybody else. I didn’t point the finger at the wrong person or people. I focused on the violators.

Unfortunately, there are victims, who blame the assault on themselves when they are attacked, raped, abused, or molested. They lose sight of what actually needs to be done in regard to exposing the person with the intent of moving on and being healed. When people deal with their pain this way, it takes them much longer to accept what happened and to heal.

There are those who get stronger based on their level of faith, and support from family and friends, despite the physical, sexual, or verbal abuse. Nine times out of ten these people use their encounters as a testimony to help others who may be experiencing the same or similar situation. They serve as a beacon of light for those who are battling this dark place.

Based on my own experience, I can plead with you to come face to face with your pain. Sadly, so many of us don't feel like we have a face that is pleasant enough to look at, simply because we now feel nasty or violated. Some people start to view and look at themselves as damaged goods. In other words, deep down inside, these people know that they were good individuals before the attack, or abuse, but the after effect makes them feel damaged emotionally and possibly mentally. Too many people who experience abuse, will try to release the pain in a negative way.

The end result causes many to run or attempt to substitute or suppress the pain. In all honesty this only makes it worse. We might go through the same pain over and over to the point where it is not pain anymore, it becomes who we are, and that is people who are full of pain. People that are full of pain become addicted and emotionally and mentally conditioned by the pain to the point that the pain consumes them. If the pain consumes them, who they were before the pain will subconsciously be erased or forgotten. This is why some people put themselves in compromising situations that got them in trouble in the first place. It becomes a repeated cycle.

But despite the pain, God is good all the time. Even though the damage is already done, God will never be done with us, as long as we are not done with ourselves. God is never the problem! Instead, He is always ready, willing, and able to provide a solution. People with anger, jealousy, pain, envy, and unresolved issues are the ones who become bad to themselves and the society we live in. You see, it took me quite a while to realize some important things about myself. Despite the pain I was able to further understand my true identity.

If you have not figured it out by now, I too was molested as a child. I'm not condoning or downplaying what happened by no means, but this violation allowed me to gain and understand my strength as a man. I chose to learn humility through my experience. It taught me how insecurities can ruin a boy as he grows into a man. It taught me to show sympathy and to give empathy to others. I would have been clueless to the dangers of sex because I was uneducated and mishandled. It could have led to a depraved mind or an uncontrolled desire that developed into a spirit of lust or perversion. A spirit that could have opened the door to certain addictions, rape, sexual harassment, etc.

I was too young to fully understand what happened to me, as well as why it happened. So, you better believe, it took me a long time to even accept my own personal pain as a reality! I too failed to identify the traumatic experience as pain. At first it felt like a very hurtful and annoying feeling that just wouldn't go away in my mind. Even as a kid I knew I shouldn't be feeling the way I was feeling. My identity was taken from me at an early age by a grown woman. This particular incident caused me to think about things that my immature mind was not ready to see or accept!

I was an innocent little boy, who was made to feel like a grown man. I battled with guilt even though I was the victim. All types of crazy embarrassing thoughts began to plague my mind. As time moved on, I began to feel like I wasn't really innocent anymore. I slowly began to feel weird, alone, and exposed. I found myself feeling naked and embarrassed! This is when I began to pray for help, guidance, and direction. Keep in mind I was only ten years old at the time. God led me to His beautiful word, which directed me to several relatable bible stories.

For example, can you imagine Adam and Eve's first reaction once their eyes were opened, and they realized they were naked. That's exactly how I felt. I was forced to come into the full knowledge of sex before I even understood what it was. I didn't possess the intellect to know what to say, how to feel, or how to respond to what was happening to me. I believe this is why it took so long to except and understand the violation. Once I accepted and was willing to understand the trauma, I was able to deal with it.

The bible played a major role in helping me to cope. It is definitely a source and guide from God to each of us. Once we read the bible with faith and accept that it is real, then and only then, will we fully understand that everything we go through in life was already written. Like my good friend Tone would always say, "There is nothing new under the sun!" It is simply a matter of going through the process of life and being blessed to live and breathe. I might be able to help you simply because I got help. What is going to happen today or tomorrow, happened to somebody else yesterday, and the day before yesterday, and so on. This is what help me to realize and see that even though I felt alone, I wasn't!

As men, a lot of us, not all, run or hide from the feelings, not realizing that it is an outlet to show us we are in pain, such as crying. Identifying your pain, allows you to identify yourself! That is the hardest or at times could be the most challenging thing to most men. It's also a very scary thing to face, simply because you have to think about it (the pain), talk about it (the pain), and constantly relive it. So, to some of us, especially the ones with the big egos, it can become overwhelming and draining. It causes many of us to feel weak. The good thing is this, it is the first step to overcoming the pain. Once you deal with it and get professional help, it will reap a good learning harvest. Times of refreshing will soon come.

So, whether you went through it or know someone who has, be sure to educate them on the importance of getting counseling, and make sure it's consistent and complete. By chance it is you, then I just gave you some homework. You know what you need to do. Handle your business. If I can fight, and get through it, so can you. We all go through difficult things in life, that are designed to help and challenge one another. When we get through it, we can educate others on how to get through.

My traumatic experience has given me the courage to write this powerful God given message to those who are stuck in limbo, denial, and severe pain. Every time I think about it, it reminds me of what other boys and girls might be going through on a daily basis. This takes me back to my childhood, that used to make me feel incredibly sad. But now when I go back to my childhood, it does the complete opposite, it makes me proud. Some of you might say proud of what? It makes me proud to know that I have overcome the violation and the pain associated with it. It makes me proud that I was able to forgive the individual. It makes me proud that I can now educate, teach, and reach plenty of people who has or will experience the same or similar trauma.

I am grateful to be in a position where I no longer harbor the pain of my past. I went through it, meaning I am no longer in that place. Our bodies are not meant to hold on to negativity. When we hold on to pain it will eventually harm us. This is why many people become bitter, commit suicide, and/or inflict pain on themselves or other people. Then you have those who suppress the pain, while at the same time trying to run from or avoid the reality of the pain. These individuals are always mad, upset, disappointed, and try to hide or isolate themselves. It is imperative that we understand that pain will never release itself. It is our job to release it before it manifests into a disease that will eventually weaken the body and possibly cause death.

# CHAPTER ELEVEN

## "Learning To Love ME"

There was a time that I strongly disliked and wasn't very fond of myself. I remember it like it was yesterday. I spent so much time blaming and criticizing myself but would uplift and defend others. It was extremely hard for me to love and believe in me. I was very insecure, which caused much of the self-inflicted pain that we've discussed in previous chapters. In most cases, when you battle low self-esteem, you really could care less about anybody else. Not me though!

The more or the less faith I had in myself; the more faith I had in others. So instead of being secure about myself and the life that I was given, I became secure about life itself and the life that everybody else was living. I loved and looked up to my father, my good friend Cisco, my cousin Ap, and my good friend Rah, to name a few. But when it came to me, I felt like an after-thought. I strongly felt like everyone else was okay with their life, their talents, and abilities, but I was uncertain and confused about mines.

Until one day I started playing basketball with my best friend Rah. Now I am not certain on what day this change transformed me into thinking and calling myself "Magic Johnson" and what made Rah think he was "Isiah Thomas", but it was a time in both our lives, especially mine, that gave me confidence and a little more faith in myself. I realized that I had certain abilities that were slowly developing.

I respected my father a lot simply because he put me on to basketball, baseball, and the sport of fighting! My father was a fighter. He wasn't afraid of anyone. His confidence level was intense. So intense that when we watched basketball, he would literally lose it and curse the players out so loud, that you would think they heard him! It would get so intense that one day after we finished watching the Yankees lose, I went outside and got into a fight with some guys in my projects. Since I was new, they would test me and always try to fight me and threaten to beat me up or jump me. So, this was normal for me.

I also remember my father being so angry with the Yankee's loss that he grabbed the bat. I never found out his intentions for actually doing that. I do know that when I came home crying telling him I had a fight, and the guys tried to jump me, but I ran, he grabbed that bat with the QUICKNESS! So, my father's attributes and characteristics helped me to want to mimic him and not disappoint him as his son. Basketball became my safe haven. It became my first love.

In many ways, basketball taught me how to love myself. We idolized our two favorite players to the point of mimicking there every move on the court. This gave me confidence, faith, and trust, in myself. I began doing things that I never thought I would be able or capable of doing.

Overtime I became a solid basketball player. This was the beginning of something great. I started having self-esteem. Being an established street basketball player continued to open many doors and avenues for me that allowed me to display and express my skills outside of basketball. You see, God showed me through Rah, Isiah and Magic that life is about confidence, friendship, inspiration, and expression.

As I began to master Magic's passes and will to win, I began to realize that it was always in me to be great at whatever I chose to master. I just needed a good friend to get it out of me, with a little inspiration of a great basketball player. If these men can express their talents and gifts to compete and win, then why can't I? I continuously watched how Magic would time and time again, will his way to a victory. I began to realize and analyze how much faith he and Isiah had in themselves. It boosted our esteem when people started calling me Magic and call Rah Isiah like we were their clones or something.

Rah encouraged me to play against some great basketball players that were considered the best in the streets. You see, good friends don't let you fail, and even if you fail, they pick you up and encourage you to try harder the next time. Rah helped to establish confidence and ability in me that I didn't even know existed. He had so much confidence he would foolishly bet on games that I felt were impossible for me to win. In the end I would prove the unbelieving side of myself wrong and win them all.

This of course expanded my ego. My confidence was at an all-time high. There came a point when I felt I could do anything I put my mind, heart, and soul too. My confidence was boosted, and my mind was transformed, to the point of me not even remembering the definition of insecurity. I slowly began to think about other talents and gifts that this new positive emotion (the spirit) was showing me. I began to ask myself, what is next. What is life after basketball?

During my spare time off the basketball court, I would find myself writing about life. As I got older and became a teenager, I realized that I was hard on myself and too easy on everyone else. When I became a young adult, I started doing some deep inner searching, which allowed me to realize that I was definitely a child of God. He created me with a specific purpose in mind. Not just to play basketball. I began to look deep into these now confident opened avenues that were being released. One of them is what I'm doing now, learning how to put my heart on a piece of paper. Not knowing that it would one day lead to me writing this book that you are now reading.

Today I have learned to express myself through writing, whether its verbal or text messages, poetry, song, or any type of communication. This has allowed me to express how I feel whether good or bad. All of this allowed me to understand that to be secure and confident should not rely on someone else. I had to love myself first, and only then it would allow me to take pride in who I am as a man.

I now strive to be what I need to be for me, without looking for something or someone else to fill the void. The only void that was there, was the void of fear, insecurity, and lack of confidence. This is the same void that challenges and destroys a lot of us. You see, this void did change me, it transformed me into the opposite of what I was.

It turned a negative into a positive. The positive aspect or emotion was this, love yourself! You cannot love yourself unless you learn and get to know yourself. You see, I couldn't love what I didn't perceive or know. Once I learned and saw what I was worth, that's when those insecure walls were broken down and replaced with confidence. I became confident enough to realize that I can't change people if I'm not changing myself. I can't believe in people unless I believe in myself. I can't fully understand people unless I understand myself.

Confidence is the key to being successful in whatever you do. If this applies, learn how to love yourself in a way that no one can ever break your confidence in you. You are destined to create and live a special life that will build and design opportunities to express you're incredible gift to the world, but most importantly to yourself. I've learned that I wasn't a waste to life, but instead I slowly became a waste to myself that created a negative deceptive mindset that had to be released from my false identity, that I alone created. The way you identify yourself will slowly shape who you believe you really are.

As I got older, I began to understand why I was so insecure in the first place. The problem was this, I allowed other people to identify who they believed I was, way before I could even fathom who I believed they were. I didn't understand myself so in return it confused me with understanding people. I started to realize that most of these people who were saying I couldn't do this, I couldn't do that, I shouldn't say this, I shouldn't say that was more confused than I was. They too, was pointing the finger at me, meanwhile ignoring themselves. The negative energy if you are around it, will transform a positive into the opposite. You see, misery loves company! What does darkness have in common with light? If someone keeps telling you something over and over every single time, they see you, what do you think will begin to be the growing result. Insecurity!

Negative thoughts, second guessing yourself and so on. I was too young to fight off too many negative insults time and time again to the point where I became all the negative things that was said about me. This is when I began to believe that I ran too slow. I believed that I was weird because I used to fight and defend myself even with teachers. I was told that I was weird because I would write about people that I cared about. I further began to believe that girls only liked me because I made them laugh. I believed that I would never be a good basketball player because I used to dribble with two hands.

But wait! Guess what happened? I became all of those things that I was told I would never be. I became a decent basketball street legend. I became a player from the Himalayas, just kidding, girls became very fond of me. I became a writer, hard worker, spiritual advisor, a father to a beautiful daughter, and whatever else God will bless me with. So, with all of that being said, those people who said those things about me were PURE EVIL!

No just kidding. The truth of the matter is most of them were going through the same things I was going thru. Kids are going to be kids. Yeah of course, some of them were jealous, some had personal issues if they even knew what that word was at the time, but most of them were insecure themselves. Children go through changes and phases in their life that will cause them to cry out or reach out in all sorts of ways. For me it was a negative, mean, and rude way at the time, but today I understand.

Now and only now, do I fully understand that for many of us, it affects us in a way that shapes our mental and emotional lives later on. Some children who tease and pick on kids grow up to be ruthless bullies whose paths become destructive and disastrous. That same destructive criticism from one individual slowly spreads throughout our communities.

Today we live in a world where one day we wake up happy, then the next day we are sad, bitter, upset, hopeless, and loss regarding what to do, how to act, or how to feel. When I was younger, I felt that life was hard, but today I realize that it's a trained mental conception, simply because life is what you make it!

# CHAPTER TWELVE

## "The School Of Life"

*How Would You Grade Yourself?*

A man's pride and ego are tested every single day. When I think of being tested quite naturally it takes me back to being in school. Every lesson we learned in school was followed by a test to ensure that we learned the lesson. As men we must realize that being tested in life isn't about passing or failing. Before you pass or fail, you must be willing to take the test. Once you finally decide, then the question becomes, "Will I pass the test?"

The truth of the matter is we can pass this test called life with flying colors. We all have the potential to ace every test, but the problem comes when we fail to study or show up in the class of life so that we can be tested. However, some of us don't want to take the test. Some of us unfortunately come to class late every day. Eventually we are all going to have to take the test whether we show up or not.

Then there are those who take the test and pass it but won't help the next man pass. Then you have a few of us who take the test, but cheat in order to pass it. Then there are the genetically gifted portion of us who could be "A" students in class but won't apply ourselves and fail to study for the test. Last but not least you have the man who thinks he's too good to take the test. This particular group could care less whether they pass or fail. We are talking about taking the test of life which as men, we face every single day that we are blessed to see and breathe.

Now we will discuss the attributes, personalities, and characteristics of men, and how we handle and deal with life on a daily basis.

**The Smart Man** – *The one who knows everything on the test but refuses to take it.*

We all know intelligent, gifted, educated, well spoken, street smart, and genetically gifted men who fail to apply themselves. This particular man has one or all of those characteristics but have nothing to show for it! I believe from my own experiences and others that the man who fails to take the test, yet possesses all of the qualifications, has an ego that is bigger than his head.

Or maybe his outer pride is leading him to believe that the test is too easy for him to even take. He believes that he's above the other students, and because of this realization or notion he doesn't need to work or apply himself. If this be the case, this particular man needs to understand why the bible says, "Lazy hands makes a man poor." Meaning, you have to go after what you want, desire, and believe in, even though you might be the most qualified.

Unfortunately, it's not going to be handed to you. Some men think that what they know is simply enough. We foolishly think in our minds that opportunities will always come to us or somebody will come knocking at our doors, begging us to take over and be in charge of the world. I don't mean to burst your bubble, but sorry guys, nine times out of ten, that's not going to happen.

Some people think that when somebody calls them lazy, they are automatically talking about physical laziness. No, I believe it starts in your mind. You train or allow your mind to become lazy first. If this is the case, then slowly but surely your body level and language will follow, causing you to be laid back and relaxed. This will prohibit you from properly utilizing, showcasing, and expressing your talents, gifts, or skills. What goes into a man's mind, body, and soul need to manifest to its completion, to perform at a level that's recognizable and noticeable in all areas.

Too many of us possess talents and abilities that tend to go unnoticed for far too long. It's unfortunate to the point where there are missed opportunities. Then other times it is just a matter of going out there and making our presence known and taking full advantage of the opportunity that may come. We need to eliminate our outer pride, and let our inner pride take over. Then we can and will pass the test and show why we are who we are destined to be! Whatever we want to do, we will be, because we took and passed the test of life. I know it sounds easy, but it takes perseverance and hard work. Sometimes we make it hard when we don't apply ourselves and refuse to take the test that will be a rewarding life changing and lifetime experience.

**The Late Man** - *This is the man that comes to class late every day.*

How many men do you know that will show up and boast and brag about showing up, like he deserves an award or something for doing it? Or he has the nerve to show up to everything late, and says, "Well at least I am here!" This particular man usually misses out on all the important things that they will eventually be tested on. These men fail to understand the importance of time. People who don't appreciate time, are all over the place, and basically never focused on the important things. Nine times out of ten, their priorities become or are already scattered.

Before this particular problem is addressed or can be fixed, this man must learn to focus on one thing at a time. If we don't learn this valuable lesson, time would have been wasted and will pass us by like the snap of a finger! If this is the case as men, we begin to complain or argue the fact that life has changed, and it didn't take us seriously, not realizing that it might have been the fact that we were the ones who didn't take life seriously. Nobody told this man to show up to work late every day or wait to the last minute to go to an important doctor's appointment.

It is not his family's fault that he missed out on his daughter's graduation, because he was trying to get his job back due to lateness. It is not his wife's fault that her family calls him the king of tardiness because he came to his brothers-in-law funeral late, knowing he was supposed to read the obituary. Or what about the time when he was supposed to be in his sister's wedding, but he showed up at the reception, missing the entire wedding ceremony even though he was a groomsman.

Now he is at a certain age where he has to play catch up with part of his life with the time that he wasted. Now he wants to apply himself and show up to class on time. He wants to take and pass the test, but unfortunately, he is so far behind, that most likely he will not pass the test. That same time that was wasted, he has to get used to studying, research and allowing himself to consider tutoring, discipline classes and inner self-control. He's now learning that it is especially important to appreciate and be on time, for the simple fact that time will not wait for you, me, or him.

In other words, time waits for no one. It doesn't matter what is going on in this world, time will continue to move on, faster than you can finish this chapter. As long as we are on this earth, we have to obey it nonstop. We are judged by and live by time and how we use it. Time consists of past, present, and future. We all have a past life, that's currently present at the moment, while the decisions we make will affect and determine our future. Life is the test. It will always present itself. As men how will we pass the test of life if we don't take it seriously?

We need to realize that our past decisions are gone, we have a chance to currently present ourselves assertively, while still setting dreams, having visions and goals, that will allow us to succeed in the future! The only way this man can and will do it, is if he shows up to everything on time focused, ready, and able with a spirit of humility. Time will not wait for this man to catch up. So, not only does this man have to continuously be on time, but he also has to be ahead of time!

Humility will allow him to appreciate the time and life that God has given him to be different.

Different first to himself, second to his family, and further to whatever life puts in his path. You might be asking; how can this man be ahead of time? Well, if you know, you have to be at work at 9:00am, you might want to get started at 7:00am. It's basically training your mind and body for future success. Preparation is key. Accountability is the key. Before making the decision to change, this man had no accountability. He didn't have a study partner or someone to push him higher. Proverbs 27:17 says, "As iron sharpens iron, one man sharpens another."

There are times when men need someone to push them out of their state of complacency and laziness, which eventually leads to ruin! Once this happens this man is now prepared to receive the benefits of passing the test of life. His ego, inner and outer pride, will now be in check. He will be able to take pride in the person he has now become and graduate from the school of hard knocks.

**The Absent Man** - *This is the man who is always absent, when it's time to take the test.*

This is the man who hardly ever shows up for anything. He rarely comes to class or school in general. He comes every once in a while. In his lost mind, he believes he can pass the test, without even coming to class consistently. This man doesn't realize that when he doesn't show up to work consistently, not going to see his kids consistently, never going to functions with his wife or girlfriend, never attending family reunions or gatherings, not going to open school night, absent when the family visits, he doesn't realize that he is mistakenly missing out on important things to learn about people and himself. He didn't realize early on that he created an image that was not attractive, personality and character wise to his family, friends, his students in class or the teachers that believed in him.

His outward approach and judgment according to people were not good. Of course, up to this point you realize that it probably doesn't matter that much what the next person is thinking outside of yourself. Well, in this case it does matter, and why? Well, it matters simply because this particular man feels something about himself that is relatable to how others view him, which means inwardly not just externally- he is a mess!

It looks like this man, will and already is failing the test of life. As men a lot of us especially this one in particular, for some reason has alienated himself from people. Someone close to him or in his class when he shows up should reach out to him and find out what's going on. Nine times out of ten something drastic, traumatic, and unfortunate happened to him in the past that allows him not to show up and be nonexistent in the class of life.

He can and will be fixed only if he opens up to someone he trusts like his best friend, girlfriend, or wife. Someone has to reach out and find out what is going on with this man inwardly? It seems like this man needs to get in touch with his feelings or try to figure out what bothered or is currently bothering him.

He needs to practice the three R's. It would appear that this type of man runs from the issues of life.

I'm sure you can relate to running in the present because of the issues of the past. We try to pretend that a particular part of our life doesn't exist. Maybe because we have continually failed, or we might be afraid of the different challenges that we might have to face. I repeat, some of us don't know how to deal with pain, so what happens is too many of us suppress or run away from it. I came to the conclusion that maybe this man didn't show up to take the test because he believes he was going to fail. His outer pride or ego most likely was telling him that he was a failure.

Something happened, or things happened in the past, that allowed this man to currently struggle with his life. Even though this happened in the past, this man has to realize that the past isn't responsible for what he does now in the present. Not dealing with the issue in the past should be a sure indication that HE is the problem and not his past. You see, the past does not recreate itself, unless you create it in your mind.

Once something traumatic happens in the past and you never properly deal with it, it will definitely deal with you in the future. An emotion is the bodies' reaction to the mind. There was built up tension in this man's body, that limited his ability to produce, and direct energy to feel the emotion, accept, and deal with it correctly. So instead of facing it and dealing with it, he instead tries to hide it or run from it. But because this particular emotion was trapped inside of him, there was nowhere to really run and hide.

Now here is the encouraging thing or the solution to this particular man. He first has to understand or realize that it is the past. At the same time because he never correctly dealt with it, it is still his current problem. He needs to be motivated, inspired, and pushed which will give him confidence to help him deal with and not run away from his problems.

Once this man gets the proper help, he will be ready to embrace his children, he will be attracted to his wife, and he will now begin to understand that you can't run away from life you have to attack it! You have to accept it. You have to study it, just like you have to study for a test in order to pass. Once he takes the test and passes it successfully, he now has an ego, but it's in check. He no longer follows the outer pride but releases his inner emotional pride.

Understand the moral to this particular example, which is, sometimes when a man doesn't show up for something, he's absent from life! Someone does not have to cry out physically, directly, or indirectly. They do not have to always be doing something that shows them crying. Its what's inside that is the most important thing. It's never what's outside. For instance, you might see a house on the outside, and it looks good, it's an incredibly beautiful looking house, but you are not going to purchase it just based on the outside of it.

You want to see how it looks on the inside. However, sometimes maybe the real estate broker or owner is not there to show you. You have to wait and see what's inside, because you do not have the key to the house. Someone else does. In the same manner, sometimes men show how they are on the outside, but will not show there insides. They have the keys to what's going on in the inside, but they will not respond, react, or release those keys to you, or anyone else. Therefore, no one knows what's going on, on the inside. But what happens is, someone gets anxious and violates or breaks inside that man's house. The man is not home so he really can't protect or defend himself.

My point is this, a lot of men do not trust people enough, to express and show there true feelings. We look at women, society, the government, and police as burglars. We are afraid that if we show our insides, we will be judged, look bad, feel weak, or feel embarrassed. If we have something in our house, that's uncommon or weird, that we do not want someone else to see or tell, we feel like they are invading our privacy. Now for all of the women that know who we really are, you all know what's really in our house.

Now this man will continue to be private unless, you allow him to feel like it is okay to open the door to his heart, or in this case house. A lot of men, that live by themselves have messy houses anyway, that need to be cleaned up. This man needs to feel comfortable with himself before he can be comfortable with anyone else. Once he understands that he has to open the door to someone to get help, he will be ready to pass and take the test of life, because he will already have all the answers.

**The Selfish Man** - *This Is The Man Who Passes The Test, But Will Not Help Others To Pass It*

There are some men who have passed the test and the class of life, and he is on his way to success, happiness, prosperity, and fulfillment. But there is one problem with this particular man. He is selfish. He refuses to join the study group and help other students, who can use his assistance. In our society we have more men who will not help, than who will. There are some though, who will give back and help, and there are others who could care less about the next man. Why is this? I would say because of their big egos, or pride. They become ungrateful and forget where they came from.

There are so many situations that I personally know regarding successful men who failed to give back to their communities. Men who will not guide or teach the next man, or even educate the youth. He will criticize, talk about, reject, and discourage the next man from accomplishing what he has accomplished. Some men will do whatever it takes to watch the next man fail the test. He will give him the wrong advice or tell him the wrong answers to the test of life. We need to understand that God created us to make the world go around, but not with money, sex, women, drugs, etc., by which society wants us to believe.

We all have the ability, creativity, and talents to help each other out in any and every way possible. We are all here for God's purpose, but we create our own purpose and begin to selfishly make it about us. When this happens, we slowly become our own keeper, instead of being our brother's keeper. This is one of the reasons why we all go through similar trials and tribulations. We are basically collectively training each other on how to overcome and pass this difficult test we call life. One hand washes the other right! Sometimes you might need to borrow something or lean on someone else.

It's funny how we are down like four flats before we find fame. Remember we all agreed that whoever made it first, would help everybody else reach their full potential of success? Unfortunately, that agreement is not always kept. This becomes the man who would rather be one of the few to make it out or get the grade, why, because he wants all the credit. He does not want anyone else to be equal to him. He wants to be in a class all by himself, why because he will probably feel threatened. His outward pride is telling him not to help the next man, but to strive to be better and more successful. He does not want any parts of competition. This is one of the many reasons why many men are labeled selfish, arrogant, sell outs, and conceited.

We can be so disconnected that we create and establish a failures mentality. This applies to those who may be failing while trying to make it in society. This particular man will see men who are succeeding and become upset, frustrated, discouraged, and confused. We become prideful and foolish to a degree and will not even approach the man for help because we feel he will turn us away.

We are convinced that he will belittle, mock, and look down on us. So, our outer pride tells us, f—k him. We continue to tell ourselves, who cares what he has, I'm good where I'm at. I am where I am because of me. I can lift my own self out of this hole. I don't need any help. I got this far by myself, why would I need help now? So, you see, we as men begin to establish this me, myself, and I mentality. Not realizing that the same man that has what we need, was helped as well. He is established because someone took the time to help him with his life test, and because he got the help he needed; he was able to pass the class. If he did not get the help, he would be exactly where we are. And even if he was fortunate enough to inherit his success, riches, or fame, it still meant that he didn't achieve it on his own.

Men! I repeat Men! Be careful not to let someone like this man, cause you to become bitter and disconnected towards yourself and mankind. Someone or something will help us to get where we need to be. There are some upcoming revolving doors and many avenues that will be opened and presented to us. "Devine things happen at divine times" is what my good friend Tone tells me. When that time comes, it is meant for us men to run and attack that ladder of success. Do not be too discouraged to the point of missing your blessing. Many of us who suffer a lot feel like in our hearts, we have a reason to be angry, upset, or mad. Still in all, it is still not a reason to not accept help when it is there.

For all of you successful men out there, I encourage you all, including myself to extend your hand to your brother or friend. Open up your hearts to give back. Be and set a good example for the youth as well as your children to follow. Always remember that anyone who gives with a cheerful and sincere heart is favored by God. Not that this alone should be our motivation to give, but God is a loving and giving and forgiving God, not counting our sins against us. That should be our motivation, for the simple fact that God does not treat us as our sins deserve, if He did, then we would not have been fortunately blessed from the very beginning.

The bible says treat others as you would want them to treat you. You will reap what you sow. You know the familiar street saying, "Karma is a bi—h!" None of us, I repeat, none of us want to be humbled by God. Most of the time, the bigger the ego, the bigger the problem(s). If we stick together more and humble our pride and egos, we could accomplish any and everything we put our hearts and minds to. We will be and establish a unit that will create an incredible community that we all will eventually be proud of. The prouder we are inwardly, the lower our egos will be outwardly.

Now let's get back to this selfish individual who regardless of what the next man is saying or doing, he is for self! This particular man still does not want anyone to be just as good as him; or to pass by him. If you go left, he will go left, if you go straight, he will go straight, if you go right, he will go right. For example, how many times have you driven on a busy highway or freeway and somebody is driving in front of you, or better yet he is way ahead of you.

He is driving at a slow pace with a lot of traffic. Now you are really not in a rush, but if you continue to drive in the left lane going 35 miles per hour in a 60 mile zone, you are going to get cursed out, beeped out, or possibly rear ended by the cars behind you. Moving forward, this driver is still driving below the speed limit, which is still causing unnecessary traffic.

You become very frustrated and at this point your patience has run out. You finally start to blow your horn several times with no changing results. So now is the time to attempt to pass this driver and leave him behind. You begin to approach the left lane to pass him, he looks in the rear view mirror and he begins to speed up, not allowing you to pass him or go into the other lane.

The point I'm making is this, a lot of men, are not in a rush, or simply do not want to go any further. But at the same time, we don't want anybody else to pass us by either. As my illustration pointed out, the man driving, was driving slowly. But the minute you began to pass him, he sped up like he was in a race for his life. Like he would have failed if he let you pass him. Once again, it's a selfish egotistical pride thing. For some weird reason as men, we sometimes feel threatened when someone attempts to catch up to whatever level we are on.

Instead of helping by moving over in another lane, we sometimes stay in the fast lane and hold people back. I can boldly say that most people that do this probably takes on that characteristic in all areas of his or life. So, I just want to encourage the men, if you are like this, take control of your pride instead of it controlling you. Lower your ego, eliminate your competitive mindset in this particular area, maybe it will help someone get pass the highway called struggles of life. Help the next man to pass the test. Do not hold someone else back for no reason.

Treat others as if you would want them to treat you. When you were late for work, remember that person that helped you, by allowing you to pass him or her by, in the busy highway we call traffic of life. We all at times need to understand or look at the big picture, the big picture that is right in front of us. We all need to create ways to help the next man understand his purpose, and why? Well, if we know our purpose, then maybe our job is to help the next man to understand or define his. Now granted, I am not saying to foolishly give our, time, money, and energy away every single day and neglect ourselves as well as our families.

Once you educate yourself, then you can educate someone else. Once you are saved, then you can save someone else. Once you are restored, then you can rebuild and restore a community. I know it is easier said than done. It sounds a little too simple right? It's all about having a solution orientated mindset. It's more about having the heart to give and love. Our egos can make this hard. Our outer pride at times makes it difficult. Our greed allows it to look farfetched. Our selfishness makes it look impossible. The truth of the matter is, it will be impossible, unless we change individually first and collectively second.

# CHAPTER THIRTEEN

## "Drugs & Alcohol Overrated"

Coping mechanisms! Sad to say, but we all have them. They vary based on what the individual is coping with. The two most common coping mechanisms, especially for men are drugs and alcohol. These vices have been a stumbling block for men and women for centuries. Yes, they are typically known for partying and making you feel good, but they are also known for helping to avoid the realities of life. I personally know many men who utilize drugs and alcohol to substitute, ignore, and hide their true intimate feelings and thoughts. Whether the user wants to admit it or not the sole purpose is to suppress PAIN!!! To drink or drug your pain away.

How many people do you know, including yourself that is or was in a conflict, crisis, argument, fight, or an unfortunate situation, that caused you to turn to drugs or alcohol. Not once, but on a consistent basis. Eventually it becomes a routine that is unavoidable. To some men, this is where the problem begins! Well, I don't know about you, but to me, the only way you can truly take your mind off of something permanently is to deal with it.

### Alcohol- Overrated

I believe a lot of men turn to alcohol for relaxation, peace of mind, or possibly, a cry for help. Do I believe when a man drinks, it can help him in certain ways, absolutely I do. However, not in the way that it's being displayed, or portrayed, lately. I believe from what I see and hear it is doing more damage, than good. For example, I see every single day on television, and hear on the radio, about DWI's, men and women killing innocent people because they are under the influence. Or I hear about or see men who destroyed their careers, and lives because of alcohol addiction. My point is, I think the positives are overrated, and I think the negatives, are underrated.

Liquor is a tool to some men who are poor communicators. There is a classic cliché, "A drunken mind speaks a sober heart!" This simply means that when you are under the influence you are subject to say anything. The word tells us to guard our hearts because out of it flows the issues of life. How can you guard your heart under the influence of flesh verses the influence of the Holy Spirit? It is impossible for the mind which is connected to the heart to concentrate, be directed, or have any form of awareness.

Alcohol affects the mental, makes you emotional and then causes you to react in the physical. The body becomes weak, and the normal response, or reaction is slow or limited. But notice how the communication is alert, sometimes clear, and aggressive, even though the mental state of mind is in a zone, and under the influence of the substance. It's almost like something inside of you is trying to come out, and will do anything to get your attention, or whoever else is there to listen. Have you ever witnessed a drunk person? They are loud, obnoxious, destructive, and uncontrollable. They reach a point where nothing matters. He will gain the courage to say whatever is on his mind or heart. Now even though this man knows he is drunk, or he is well on his way to reaching that level, he still continues to be or act the way he feels. To him, it's a good feeling of expression, and relaxation. Whatever was going on before he was under the influence, is now secondary. His number one priority right now is getting his drank on.

Quite naturally you can't tell this man that his drinking is out of control. Others may notice it and be genuinely concerned, but he will be in denial. He feels since he doesn't get involved with too much conflict, drama, or any unfortunate circumstances when he drinks or is heavenly under the influence that he is good. Keep in mind though, the only time this man drinks, is when he has an issue, conflict, or major argument. Some of his predicaments and situations are big, and some of them are small. The ones that are big, and when he turns to the liquor, he feels like it's okay, because it is only a few drinks to keep his mind off the issue. In his mind, he is doing it so that he won't go or do something crazy. So, basically his few drinks calm him down. It keeps him from making a drastic, out of control, rash, emotional decision.

Many men, deal with their situations and circumstances the same. Instead of exposing and expressing ourselves to our, girlfriends, children, friends, wives, family, etc., we choose to expose ourselves to a substance. Instead of expressing what's on our minds, we allow our minds to be influenced and dragged further away from ourselves and our people and closer to the preferred substance. And speaking of closer, a lot of men, especially this one, is starting to have a deep, compassionate, intimate, communicative relationship with the alcohol. He subconsciously loses himself in the bottle.

## Best Friends With The Substance

A lot of men develop deep patterns, hobbies, interests, devotion, and love for certain things. There are very few things that we will admit that we are close too. So, it's almost like picking, taking out, or pulling teeth, when it comes to us, exposing or expressing our feelings, or deep thoughts. So most of us, will release, expose, or confess what's on our hearts, and minds, in a secluded place.

We will become vulnerable in the weirdest places, with the weirdest people, doing the weirdest things. Or sometimes, we may find ourselves reaching or crying out without recognizing it. In my opinion I feel like this demonic stronghold not only kills many men, but destroys their lives, breaks up families, and breaks down the body. This spirit also causes the man to become brainwashed into thinking they are good while they are destroying everything within their circle. In the event he does recognize that he is out of control, he has the capacity to become self-centered and thinks he is only hurting himself.

Unfortunately, we treat this substance like it's our best friend. Like it has our best interest at heart. Some of us even try to use it as a motivator to reach higher levels in life. We go on a date with it, every Friday and

Saturday night. Some of us take it out on weekdays, even if it compromises our family time. When we are mad, upset, discouraged, disappointed, or depressed, who do we run too? We run to it. Instead of us running to our friends, girlfriends, wives, therapist, pastors, or God. When we go on vacation, who do we take with us? Even if we leave it at home, we don't panic, because we will find another way to get it. Alcohol is everywhere!

We don't even have to look for it. Most times it will look for and find us. When it finally catches up to us, it will damage and hurt us, inside and out. And when it hurts us, who do we blame? We blame ourselves, or everybody else, instead of blaming the substance. We don't get mad at it, we get mad at us, we take it out on something, or somebody else. We are faithful to it, we are devoted to it, and we will never cheat on it, even though it's not faithful to us. We will put it, before everything, and everybody. It is highly overrated, but at the same time, underestimated.

We give it too much power, not realizing that it's limited. Realistically, the only power it has, is the power we give it. It has no power, until we release, or open it. Once we release and open it, then it will try to influence, and open our minds. It influences not just a man, but men, and other people. It hangs out with everybody that's willing to give it a try. It's very versatile and flexible. It desires to be with you or go wherever you take it. Its sole purpose is to entertain you, by any means necessary. Sadly, some of as men can't do without it. It's like a thorn in our flesh.

It calls out to some men at all times of the night, especially, when we have unfortunate situations, such as death in the family or a bad break up. Don't let the stress of life take over, most men definitely run to the bottle when this happens. It knows you are in pain, upset, confused, and vulnerable. That's when it will penetrate the heart and mind for the routine attack. It doesn't care what you are doing, who you are with, or where you are at. It calls everywhere - at churches, schools, work, it even makes house calls. Just like you have a family, well so does it.

It has friends and family, who are willing to serve you. As long as you have the money, it will accompany, your, heart, mind, and soul. It comes in all different flavors, some are strong, and some are light. The choice is yours. Even though it can make you feel like you don't have one. You can run towards it, or you can run away from it. If you choose to run towards it, it will persuade, instruct, and question your mind, as it gets to know you. It will begin to speak, and I do mean very loudly. It will ask questions like...

Do you want to feel good?

Do you want to be in a trance or a zone?

Do you want to forget about your problems?

You should be asking yourself...

Do you want a hangover?

Do you want to embarrass yourself?

No matter what it will still manipulate you into thinking that you are shining, being expressive, talking to it, crying to it, spending money on it, and most of your time on it. This substance will have you thinking you are gaining temporary relief. It will make you feel invincible. The sad thing is once you lose yourself in the alcohol, you have little to no recollection of what you did previous to drinking. You might consider this your best friend, your hang out buddy, your consultant, or your confidant. It considers you another target of the enemy.

This so called friend that you have become co-dependent on doesn't really care about you. It is only a temporary fix and can only destroy and hinder every area of your life. Once the destruction has manifested, the cycle continues with the next man and the next. I mean lets be real, alcoholism has been around for centuries. Even Noah got drunk after they exited the boat, so I understand but it doesn't make it right.

Let's take a look at some other scenarios!

**Scenario One:** The brother who has a lot of money, no friends, marital problems, and is stressed to the max. What do you think he is going to do? Hit the bottle of course! He sees that as his only option not to feel or to deal.

**Liquor speaking:** *Maybe I will influence him to take me to his job. He can sneak me in his locker. He is about to get fired anyway. My cousin Hennessey told me last week, he almost got himself fired. He was deeply under his influence and cursed his supervisor out.*

**Scenario Two:** *What about my son, Absolute, did you hear what happened, Absolute, almost absolutely took home boy out. He was driving, while he was under his influence, and nearly crashed into a tree. He just missed it by two inches.*

**Liquor Speaking:** *Only time will tell, whether he will open me up again, and allow me to explore his insides. But keep in mind, he has a lot of family and* *friends, and even if he doesn't buy me or release me from this bottle, maybe his family or friends will. They are all genetically, alcoholic people anyway. I am just waiting patiently, holiday season is around the corner, labor day, thanksgiving, Christmas, and Halloween. Those are the most stressful let's get drunk holidays, or celebrations, so I know I will be able to influence somebody's brain to take a taste. And by the way, speaking of taste, I have a taste for some liver, I would love to tear some man's liver up. That's where we do the most damage.*

By no means am I making fun of or mocking men who drink or who are addicted to alcohol. I just want the men and women to understand from a different level what the liquor can do to your mind, body, and your entire life. I just want people to understand that to release your emotional anger, stress, agony, and pain to alcohol, could and most likely will be devastating to you as a whole. So be careful not to treat the bottle like it's your reliable, trustworthy, best friend. If you don't have someone to talk to, or to confide in, then get on your knees and pray to God for strength, faith, endurance, grace, sympathy, and support, to overcome the battles of alcohol addiction.

Release the pain of everything and everybody to your Creator. If you are an addict, only God can truly help you to overcome it, anyway. Whether He personally touch's your heart, or works through advisors, programs, councilors, or special people that He placed in your life. Submit your pain and prayers to Him, He will relieve and restore you. He will help your insecurities, failures, short comings, character flaws, immaturity's, etc.

I have said this before, and I will say this again. I am not a religious person, nor am I condemning or trying to sound like one. However, I do believe in God, and my bible tells me that believing is not enough, if you practice what you preach, or if you are what you talk about, then you will know the truth, and the truth will set you free. And how will you know the truth unless you examine or practice it for yourself. That's exactly what I am trying and striving to do. My goal in life is to serve God, and God only. I cannot serve God if I don't follow Him. And I cannot follow Him fully, unless I know Him, which is exactly my point.

Get to know God, and then you will understand and know yourself. My goal is to get closer to Him, more and more, every day. I really feel and believe that if we fought more to have a personal relationship with God in our society, there would be less DWI'S, less alcoholics, less drug addicts, less suicide cases, etc. This is one of the reasons why I wrote this book. I want to encourage, motivate, and inspire men to continue to seek, and to establish a real, deep, passionate, relationship with God.

My desire is that men stop being afraid of having or establishing a relationship with God. We definitely need to fear God, but not in the way that some men do. Some of us fear God when we are in trouble. One of the first thoughts that comes to a man's mind is, when he is in trouble to the point where he feels like his life depends on it is, "Oh my God! What have I done to deserve this situation that will probably destroy my life?"

Then, this man begins to think of all the bad things he did to people and, in his heart, he feels like God is punishing him. So, this man becomes frightened by God. Not realizing that God can destroy us at any time, and probably would have done it a long time ago if He chose to. On the contrary, He just wants us to be encouraged and influenced by Him. He is trying to get our attention away from the influence of drugs and alcohol, or any kind of influence that will eventually entice us away for good. He wants us to get close to Him, and further away from the addiction, or influences of drugs and alcohol.

## Drugs Underrated

If alcohol is overrated, then drugs are underrated. I say underrated, due to the effects it has on your mind, body, and life. Now we discussed the destructive impact of alcohol and though they are both mind controlling substances; drugs carry a greater level of destruction. As we have discussed thus far in this book, men go through a lot of sh-t and as previously stated we all respond differently. Some men turn to women, some become workaholics, some commit suicide, but others turn to drugs. The drugs cause men to become numb, bored, arrogant, egotistical, selfish, or ignorant to what is really going on with us, or to what we have become.

All of this causes pressure, and many men can't handle the pressures of life. Therefore, before we flip out, we result to weed, pills, lean (syrup), wet, and any other mind altering substance that will temporarily lift the pressure. To be honest no one is exempt. Even the riches people have turned to drugs to deal with the pressure of pain, so this isn't just for men who are broke, busted, and disgusted. Drugs effect people from all walks of life. They do not discriminate against race, social status, financial status, or age. Drug abusers are getting younger and younger with each generation. The unfortunate thing about drugs is the deception of thinking it's not a problem. Like alcohol, it is very manipulative and cunning.

There are many successful people who are avid drug users, and they have the audacity to label themselves as being functioning addicts. Which means it doesn't interfere in their careers or social life. This is demonic deception in the worse way. Again, it goes back to the emotional pain that has been buried and using drugs and alcohol is their delusional way of thinking they are safe from the past. When people turn to drugs their issues could be spiritual, physical, mental, a false sense of reality, identity issues and much more. We must be careful of the self-sabotaging spirit that wants to take us out as men.

It is important to check our egos at the door or suffer the consequences later on in another room. We cannot let the room that's nicely designed, flawlessly decorated, perfectly painted, with beautiful pictures on the wall, and shiny floors to have cracks in the roof. That is a disaster waiting to happen. This room is your lifestyle. This is why, sometimes it's not good to have everything that you want. Because after you get everything that you want, then you don't understand and realize what you really need. Or you might forget about what you need, because you might be focused too much on what you want. Which most of the times will cause you to be confused on the difference between a want and a need. And unfortunately, the greatest example that I can use, is the need and the desire to use drugs.

For some men, and people in general, we might see drugs as a want. When it's all said and done, it turns into a need, which is really not a need. The desire for drugs was at first a want. This want could be based on influence. Since you have not experienced it yet, you think its harmless. It only takes one time to get hooked. It only takes one time to experience that I don't care about anything feeling and it's a wrap. What you thought you wanted for most now becomes a dire need.

Sometimes we allow our minds to deceive and play tricks on us. Now keep in mind, your mind might be playing tricks on you before it gets influenced by drugs. Just imagine what it will be like once it's introduced to the preferred substance. And if you are well off, with money, power, etc., then you will probably feel more convinced to do you, without taking the same precaution that somebody will take that has little.

All men don't fall in this category, but sadly, most of us do. The more success we have, the more problems we have. I have witnessed drugs take so many people out that it's almost like the norm. To me it has changed dramatically.

Some men in the beginning, don't really know the effects or even have a clue of what drugs can really do to them. It's not until the drug abuse becomes dangerous that there is a cause for alarm. Then we start to understand. We no longer assume that he or she is okay because they say that they are, have what they have, look like what they do, know what they know, or that they are who they are. We begin to understand that it affects everybody. When we reach certain statuses in life, we tend to feel untouchable and this causes men to become complacent, arrogant, egoistical, prideful, conceited, lost, or bored and these things causes many to flirt with drugs. That introduction leads to personal, spiritual, emotional, mental, and sometimes physical death.

Most drug abusers start abusing their bodies, brainwashing their minds, ignoring, or running away from the spirit, and selling their souls. You might ask, substituting, ignoring, and selling thier souls to what? To drugs and alcohol. The truth of the matter is drugs can break a man down faster than the almighty dollar can. Why because, all it takes is you mishandling, not budgeting, giving away, or just simply making bad decisions, concerning your money when it comes to drugs. Some men who are wealthy, use their money for power, control, authority, as a useful tool to get those drugs by any means necessary.

The bible tells us that the spirit is willing, but the flesh is weak. My brothers there is nothing wrong with being weak in the flesh, because God will strengthen you. There are so many of our brothers and sisters who are strung out on crack cocaine, handlebars, wet, weed, and syrup. Marijuana is a billion dollar industry, but it is killing our men, women, and children every day. It is hindering men from being fathers and law abiding citizens of society. Just imagine the prison population that is filled with brothers who either sold drugs or consumed them.

Think about the motherless and fatherless child(ren) who are fending for themselves because their parents have been locked, chained, and imprisoned by dope to cope. Like I said drugs are underrated! We witness the destruction on the mind, but we think it's cool because we are trying to calm the soul. This deceptive trick of the enemy is killing, stealing, and destroying good men and women who were born with promising futures.

I'm sure you are saying, "Charlie, you just don't get it?" I beg to differ! I understand the pain! I understand the struggle! I too was molested! I too battled with insecurities! I too have experienced some hardships and rough patches in life, but I learned to give it to God. By no means am I saying I am innocent of indulging in these substances, but one day I woke up and realized it wasn't working. They were working me! They were creating a beast that I wasn't proud of and that is what happens to most men.

We allow other things to turn us into the opposite of who God created us to be. When do we stop allowing pain to be the driving force of our existence? God told Cain before he killed his brother Abel, that sin was knocking at the door and if he chose to open that door sin would consume his life. Cain opened that door, and the end result was murder. He murdered his brother in cold blood because of his uncontrolled emotions. When you smoke a blunt, smoke the pipe, pour up the purple stuff, or pop pills you are opening the door to not only kill yourself, but the possibility of killing others. Just think about the number of people who hurt someone under the influence, but when they sobered up, they had no recollection of the incident.

Come on my brothers and my sisters, it's time to sober up. It's time to find healthier ways to cope with your pain. It's time to release the pain of your past and look forward to a brighter future. There is greatness on the inside of YOU! I'm not saying you can drop a habit overnight, but when will you choose life over death and prosperity over poverty. The victory over drugs and alcohol was won over two thousand years ago on the cross.

I'm not trying to church you to death or come off as a holy roller, because I have flaws too. The purpose for this book was to reveal some true wisdom and knowledge regarding our lives as men, because truth be told, we get a bad rep most of the time. Open your heart and hear the words of the prophetic flow.

**Prophetic Flow**

> *Woe to the man who can't handle success because success will surely handle him. Woe to the man who is stressed, and he slowly allows the drugs to dismantle him. It overtakes him, until he's out of breath, it will only break him, until nothing is left. Do you still believe he is blessed? Will you pray that he is put to rest? Will God still take him, will we learn or be next, will you burn, or pass the test? Will you yearn to be your best, or will the substance take him, how can you rebuild, or remake some, learn to give more, and receive less, open your heart, and throw away the fake one, it's not a skill,*

*that we allow the drugs to kill, from the very start, it will do what it feel, and rip us apart, do you really believe, that it's that smart, are you still deceived to think you are ok, or do you still receive, because you pray, do you think you have a lot of time because you wake up every day. Time will wait for no one, neither will the liquor, it will eat you alive, faster than quicker, but you are still fooled by the success that you achieve, totally losing yourself, continuously missing the picture and the lies you believe. If the mind is a terrible thing to waste, then why waste it, if you are in so much pain, then why not face it, you continue to hide behind the alcohol, instead of getting on your knees, and begging God please, relieve me of this pain and make at ease, instead you wait for the rain that allows you heart to go up and down on that same trampoline, how do you explain yourself if you are confused, how could you blame yourself if you have no clues. How can you game yourself without playing the game, how can you regain your wealth?*

# CHAPTER FOURTEEN

## "Is Sex The Solution?"

The topic of sex for many can be both controversial and sensitive. Sex serves many purposes, yet most of the purposes have been distorted by the world's view of sex. Yet, we must understand that sex was created by God. It is extremely hard to understand or use wisdom when you are lacking knowledge on any subject.

We as mankind have perverted sex and therefore taken the original intent to a whole different level. The foundational purpose of sex according to the word of God was and still is "to be fruitful and to multiply" which means to create life. This is the original purpose for sex. Outside of creating life, sex is to be pleasurable between a husband and a wife. This is where the spirit of perversion manifests because the world condones sex before marriage.

I myself was introduced to sex entirely too early and it was through a violation which created a spirit of perversion to manifest in my life. This caused a great deal of pain and confusion for me. This robbed me of the opportunity to have a healthy sex life. I was robbed of the choice to choose the young lady I would lose my virginity to. At some point I pondered the following questions:

*Was I confused about sex from the beginning?*
*Did sex hurt me, or did it help me?*

You might be wondering how sex could help or hurt. I believe that when we are exposed to certain things too early, it is a means of preparation for later in life. In layman terms you have to encounter a test, to have a testimony. What I encountered was unfortunate and wrong, but it prepared me to focus and get in touch with my sexuality as a young boy. On the flip side, as I got older I began to realize how much it affected me as a teenager concerning the opposite sex. I felt weird, insecure, and strange. It was extremely hard for me to face as an adult. This is when I realized that sex is not the number one solution for men.

There are several men who might fight me on this. Some might think I have an issue with women. Some might wonder if I even enjoy sex after being violated and the answer is yes. I am not knocking sex. I'm simply enlightening you as my brother in regard to how we use sex as a coping mechanism to deal with life. I have learned to appreciate what sex is really about. I understand today that if sex is not handled properly, it can affect and/or destroy part if not all of your life.

There are plenty of men whose lives have been destroyed by sex. These men have been tricked by the enemy to believe that sleeping with multiple women, committing adultery, watching porn, and masturbation are okay. When life gets tough the first thing most men think about is releasing pressure through sex. Don't get me wrong I am not saying this is wrong, I am simply saying this isn't the only solution. When do we take the time to get out of the flesh, to walk in the spirit?

When do we invite God in and give Him the opportunity to help us relieve the pressures of life? There are some men who go to great lengths to have sex with women. They will give up money, gifts, houses, cars, etc.., but once the few minutes is over the woman is tripping looking for more material possessions and the issue you had before sex is still waiting to be handled. It is important to learn how to do sex Gods way. When I was violated, what did I do? I prayed and I was only ten. So, come on brothers it can't be that hard to ask God how to handle life the right way.

Just think about it! If we were doing sex God's way, would there be so many sexually transmitted diseases in the world. Would there be men and women infected with herpes, AIDS, Chlamydia or HPV? Would there be so many dead beat dads, who can lay down and create children, but not take care of them? Would there be so many rapists and child molesters who have to be labeled in society as pedophiles? Would there be so many babies having babies? To answer these questions, NO! There would be balance and order in the earth. Sex again would be used for creating life and pleasure for married men and women.

**Poetic Flow**

*Sometimes a man's heart is beating, but his brain is dead. His sex game is tight, but his mind is loose. His money is stable, but his penis is everywhere. His heart is worried, but in his mind he doesn't care. Would he be able to do whatever it takes? Will he learn from all the mistakes that he makes? His morals are good, but his motives are bad, woman, are you with him, because you are discouraged or sad. Or is it the best sex you ever had. To a woman his ego may be huge, but his penis is small, will you help him to win, but runs when he falls. Will he fall into sin, or change and give his all? A good father is a blessing, but a bad one is a curse, in the end will he stand tall, or will he put himself first.*

Now, I want to speak to the women! First and foremost, you were fearfully and wonderfully created by God. Our bodies, both male and female are the temples for the Holy Spirit. You are a Daughter of God. That makes you royalty, which is why you have the queen, and you have the king. Women you were created to be treated with honor and respect. You were also created in the image and likeness of God. You were formed from the man's rib. You weren't even formed from the dirt. That speaks volumes. Yet many of you allow yourselves to be mistreated, misrepresented, and abused. This was and is NOT God's will for your life. You must learn your value, before anyone else can value you.

You shouldn't be so thirsty for a man that you sleep with him based on his looks or because another girlfriend said he was good in bed. It's time to stop this cycle of dysfunction where you sleep with a man because you are afraid to lose him. You have no idea what type of man he is, but you marry him and end up being abused, dogged out, and left emotionally dead. Stop having sex to cure loneliness, because trust me, after the sex is over and he leaves, the loneliness will still be there.

Sex doesn't cure emotional trauma; it only makes it worse. Why? Because when you have sex based on emotions and not facts, you end up on an emotional roller coaster and this ride is hard to get off because it never stops until the individual stops it. Some women and men thrive off of this temporary thrill, but it is damaging.

Can you imagine the number of men and women who are walking around bitter, angry, resentful, and rejected because of emotional sex? Instead of taking the time to love ourselves, to deal with our truth, and get whole, sex becomes the Band-Aid, especially for us men. Women many of you need to realize, that you are hurting us more than you are helping us. There is a lie floating around that only women get emotionally attached during sex, but this is a lie from the pits of hell. Men tell the truth, we get emotionally attached too.

We try to act like we are hitting and quitting, but that female is on your mind whether you want to admit it or not. Yes, it might look like we are not attached because we can sleep with multiple women at one time. A soul tie is a soul tie! You can't sleep with a person and not be attached. When God created sex, it was meant to be with one person. That is why the bible says the man will leave his father's house and cleave to his wife. Sex in the natural is what creates the spiritual union in the sight of God. When we have sex with a man or woman, we create a soul tie. Your soul is now connected to the person you slept with. Therefore, it is impossible to truly hit it and quit it. The two souls have connected and become one. This is why we must be careful who we connect with. We actually take on that individual's spirit.

There are men who are addicted to sex, especially the bachelors, which we use as an excuse to have sex with different women. It makes us feel emotionally and mentally secure. For some of us, it creates an ego boost. It allows the ego to feel superior! It makes us feel like we are doing nothing wrong. We tell ourselves we are good because we aren't in a committed relationship. We convince ourselves that we don't have to commit to one woman, therefore we can have sex with whoever we want. Well guess what happens in society when a large portion of men think this way? We become fathers who are not committed to the relationship.

This is why so many men are on child support and are labeled as deadbeat dads. There are so many men sitting in prison because they refused to pay child support because it was never their intention to make a baby. It was supposed to be a one night stand, that turned into an eighteen year prison sentence to some men. To be honest how can many of us expect to be good fathers, if we don't have the desire, attributes, and characteristics, of being committed.

We need to learn the value of thinking before we react. Sex is permissible, but it's not always beneficial. If you know you are not ready to commit to being a father, or to the woman you are with, then either don't have sex or protect you and the woman. If she gets pregnant, there is a possibility for regret. You may not regret having the child, but the woman who you are having the child with. Sex is not something that should be taken lightly.

There are a lot of consequences that can result in disaster, heartache, and constant pain. Pain that becomes emotional, physical, spiritual, and mental. Your mind will make you believe that sex is something you need consistently as a man. That's when the beauty and the joy of sex become a self-fulfilled desire that leads to an addiction. I believe a large portion of men have no clue how we let sex control our emotional, mental, and spiritual wellbeing.

There are some brothers who feel it's not fair that there are so many gorgeous, beautiful, gifted, smart, intelligent women in this world; not to look, stare, get to know, and have sex with. We think and feel like God created them for us. We feel like there shouldn't be so many rules, regulations, laws, and restrictions when it comes to being with them.

So, we ignore the restrictions, or we begin to slowly create our own. When we create our own, things mess up, or blow up in our face. Then we realize why there are standards, boundaries, rules, and regulations. I hate to say this but there are some brothers who even feel like we have been set up to lose in life, because we are outnumbered by the women. Well, the bible did say there would be seven women to one man. It's so many of them, that it's impossible to neglect, ignore, keep it moving, turn down, and reject. Especially if they seduce, initiate, follow, flirt, or pursue us.

Some men have even been raped by a woman then boast and brag about it, like it's okay. But remember if we rape them, we are rapist, and are going to jail. But if they rape us, we get laughed at and praised. If you tell a man that you got raped by a woman, he will say, "Yo, that's what's up! You are the man! Was it good?" On the flip side of the conversation, in reverse, the questions should be, "Did you at least wear a condom? Did you go check yourself out? Do you remember what happened? Were you drunk or high? Who is this woman? Where is she from? Does she do this often? How do you feel?" Men have feelings too I don't care how much we try to play hard.

Women are emotional, yet men cry too! The evil one sets us up to lose, but God sets us up to win. The evil one is somewhere, God is everywhere. The evil one is deceitful and bad; God is righteous and good. The evil one is temporary, but the God Almighty is forever. Both of them will set you up, day after day, year after year; the question is, "Which one will you follow?" Are you going to represent God or the enemy?

If you define sexual intercourse you will see partnership, compatibility, a communication between a man and a woman. The same communicated bond that God gave us in Christ. God created intimacy for us to enjoy sex the right way, unfortunately we sometimes get enticed to lean towards the wrong way, which becomes sin. When I say sin, I am talking about, Adam and Eve who realized they were naked, so they hid themselves.

Well, if you think about it for a moment, they hid themselves because they were exposed to their naked bodies for the first time, which caused them to automatically feel a certain kind of way. They felt guilt, fear, and spiritually separated! This is why sin separates us from God. Obedience to God keeps you spiritually grounded, protected and on the right path or direction. But when we go in another direction that's not God's will, we miss the mark because we are no longer following Him. Since God is loving, gracious, and merciful, we might get another opportunity, we just have to wait for it to come around again.

God wants us to win, but there may be some losses along the way. God created women for us! He created them to walk side by side with us. He created them to support us and to create outside versions of ourselves in the form of children. Isn't God awesome! The only problem is many men fail to see it this way. We want to sow our royal oats when we can have it all with just one. Proverbs 18:22 says, "He who finds a wife, finds a good thing and obtains favor from the Lord." Wouldn't you prefer favor or female fans. While you are thinking you are God's gift to women. They are the gift provided for us. Adam was originally in the garden alone. Just him and the animals. How would you feel today being in a world full of animals and no women?

You wouldn't like that at all. Which means we have to learn to appreciate God and His consideration of our needs as men. Sex is a want outside of a commitment, but a need inside of a marriage. God is mindful of us and everything pertaining to us. He knows our needs and has graciously supplied them, but we can't be greedy and unappreciative either. The real problem is some of us want them all. We are not satisfied with one. It doesn't matter if we are married or not God sets us up to have our own wife to marry. Our marriages turn into a curse, when we decide to go outside of the marriage, and then only God can fix it. But before we let God fix it, we get mad at Him, like He forced us to marry.

God didn't tell us to cheat. He didn't tell us to lust after every woman, who we think want us. He didn't tell us to get multiple women pregnant that we are not committed to. Truth be told the only person who sets us up is - US. We set ourselves up to lose and when we lose, God is the one who bails us out, with His true plan to win, by which we should have followed from the beginning.

Many times, we fail to see the victory that God has for us, because we are not thinking about God or the women. We are not even thinking about ourselves. Sometimes, we are not even thinking. We are letting our sexual desires think for us. We begin to think with our private parts or allow them to think for us. Failing to realize that our private parts (men and women) are not even thinking about us. They can't protect us; we have to protect them. Do you really think it's concerned about a woman's personality, or a woman's character? Do you really think it cares about how she feels, or how small or big her heart is? It's more concerned about how small or big her butt or breast are. Don't follow the FLESH, the flesh is always weak.

Speaking of weak, sex nearly destroyed my emotional, mental, physical, and spiritual state of being. I am eternally grateful to God that it didn't destroy me. I was able to overcome it, at least for a long period of time. I had to make some drastic changes in my thinking. I had to keep my feelings under control. I had to control and keep my physical needs in order, and last but not least, I had to keep it spiritual.

I started being disciplined, by setting some major dreams and goals. I set the bar extremely high for myself. I knew that the only way I could possibly deal with this sex thing was to battle it face to face. I had to have an enormous amount of faith to do the unthinkable. I decided to practice abstinence. I became totally celibate at the age of twenty and I was celibate from 1995-2000.

I know some of you are probably thinking, yeah right! I was sex free for five long years. It was more of a disciplined, spiritual thing for me. I tested myself. I wanted to see, how long I could go without sex. Believe you me, I didn't think I could last five days, let alone five years. Because of my new commitment, conviction, and devotion to God, I achieved it. I learned discipline, patience, endurance, faith, and character.

I learned how to be a fearless mature man of God. Plus, it also helped me understand Charlie. As well as, allowed me to understand that sex can be disciplined, controlled, and when the time is right, enjoyable. It helped me to realize how strong I was, especially when I relied on God. It also helped me to realize that it is an ongoing life challenging thing. But to each its own, whatever works for you.

I was considered weird by many because I chose to do the right thing for me. It amazes me how off our thinking can be when it comes to doing the right thing verses the wrong thing. I'm not knocking them, everybody has their own time, conviction, or lot in life. The direction they might go in, or not go in, is between them and God. I try my hardest not to judge anyone. However, the bible commands me to view, look, see, and to judge what is right. It's not about people, it's about God. How, when, and why, does He view and look at sex the way He does? The truth of the matter is people don't believe I accomplished that goal with discipline and control because sex controls most of them. They don't discipline the sex; the sex disciplines or controls them. They are addicted to it. They desire to have it, daily, some, at any means necessary.

Sex can be an enjoyable gift from God, or it can be a painful curse, directed and led by satan. Sex is compassionate, loving, and intimate, but it can also be heartless, selfish, dreadful, and evil, to the point of producing death. Sex can be an open easy target but can easily become a very dark secret. Sex can be your best friend or your worst enemy. Sex can be peaceful to the heart but can deceive and hurt a lot of feelings.

## Sex Affects Environment, Culture, Society and Bodies

The consistent need for sex will eventually turn into lust, that causes an undisciplined routine, that's if not protected will produce a human life. We produce this life with no major commitment, or devotion, that creates a continuous cycle that is passed on from generation to generation. The bible states in many scriptures that the body was not meant for sexual immorality with numerous partners.

This is called fornication. We are not meant to have sex with multiple women. This causes us to become emotionally confused and eventually we become addicted to the confusion. Instead of breaking out of this confusion, we continuously perform the same sexual activities which further damage our minds and put our bodies at risk. This of course becomes a cultural thing that will affect our little precious seeds! You are probably asking what are precious seeds? They are the children that God blesses us with. Key words are "God blesses" because we can't create without Him.

Sometimes our undisciplined, irresponsible ways affect us, as well as our children. A lot of irresponsible men and women are undisciplined when it comes to sex. We need to learn how to break the cycle, instead of being a part of it. It starts with us thinking about more than ourselves, which can cause a lot of negativity in our life. To me, there is nothing negative about having a child, or children. In fact, in Genesis 1:27-28 it says, "For God created male and female, He blessed them and said, be fruitful and increase in number."

With that being said, or according to my bible, have all the sex you want as long as we do it His way. God created it for us to increase and grow on this earth in a positive way. But of course, we know where there is a positive, there is potential for a negative, trying to trip you up! Here is where the children get entangled into our negative mess. The negative manifest based on the irresponsible root of how the child was conceived. Plus, the lack of devotion, and commitment, after the child is born. There are necessary sacrifices that need to be made for these children. There is unity that should be created between the parents for the sake of creating healthy children.

When we as parents, fail to have these attributes, or characteristics the beautiful blessing starts to look like an irresponsible and uncontrolled curse. I say uncontrolled because you would think that most men would learn from their mistakes, or silly undisciplined ways. Instead, some men get worse, and instead of fixing the damage we caused, we create, and consistently cause more damage. We add fuel to the fire. We relive or reopen the wound. We create or establish a routine of the same mistake that forms into a pattern and leads to addiction.

We become addicted to the sex, yet run from the responsibilities, commitments, and consequences of it. This is again another example of missing the mark, or sin! And by the way, I am not just talking about the men, I am talking about the women as well. I am talking about the women who are sexually active in an uncontrolled way, where it appears that every year, they are popping out babies, not having a clue, who the baby father is.

Having a child does not make you men or women. It doesn't even make you a mother or a father. Understanding, teaching, and being a student of the responsibility of raising a child gives you the authority to be labeled as a mother or father. It is important for both the men and women to grasp this concept because most times it's mamas' baby and daddy's maybe, especially in the African American culture. The man was eager to release his pressure, yet not man enough to stand under the pressure of being a father to his children.

**Poetic Flow**

*Some men run, some men hide, some will give, and some will provide. Some identities are real, some are fake. Some will give, and some will take. Some will fall, and not give up; some will rise, and stand back up. Some will have faith, and go after what they believe, some will under, and overachieve. Why is it so hard for you to believe, that some will still neglect and abandon what she will conceive? A baby is a beautiful thing, why waste it, if the water is poison, then why taste it? If sin kills, then why pursue it, if you knew it was wrong, then why you do it. Say what you mean, and mean what you say, if you don't believe in God, then why do you pray. When you are in trouble, who is your protection? Will you believe in a curse, or will you accept the blessing? Are you looking for the answer, before the question, or are you confused or lost, with no direction? Do you abuse the cost, not being prepared for the lesson? Do you choose to be the boss, with no heart or affection? You are a fool if you are still lost, still second guessing. You are still waiting for the answer, without understanding the question or the lesson. If God is in your heart, then why are you still looking, you continue to fall apart, without the spiritual blessing of cooking, if the food is good, then eat it that's a start, if you have caused trouble, begin to start your confession, which is very intelligent or smart. Be real to thyself and love your seed, a beautiful baby is a blessing is what the bible reads. God paints the perfect picture His incredible art, some will live to give, but others will die in greed. Some will dress to protect the flesh, but still will bleed, still with no direction, it's like trying to finish a race before we even start, if that's not the case, then the question is still, why you still falling apart and continuing to bleed. Are you still saying God knows my heart, allowing and confusing your mind to build that deceitful seed?*

The question still stands...Is sex the solution? Is it the solution to your pain, suffering, loneliness, problems, issues, lust, desires, insecurities, and short comings of life? Is it the solution to your pleasure, friendships, relationships, marriages, children, and sinful pain? I don't know any of your lives, so I will allow you to answer these questions for yourselves. My prayer is for people to think and be wise before they engage in sexual relationships with anyone, especially if you are not married, and want kids, or don't want kids. Don't consciously bring an innocent child into dysfunction.

It is very unfortunate that I have seen more negatives, than positives, in my forty plus years on this earth, when it comes to relationships that are sexual, with children included. A real true man that is in touch with his sexual needs, and sexual side, will tell society; to go back to the pits of hell and take their brainwash-

ing beliefs with them! A real man who wants a family, with a QUEEN, not a worldly woman. A real man who wants to build a family, and be the head over his family, and lead them to God! He will instruct other men who are afraid to commit and devote himself to God. HE WILL VOICE THESE THREE WORDS...
Wake up men!
Wake up men!
WAKE UP MEN!!!!!

Be willing to make the change and be the change that is needed in the world, for God gave man dominion over the earth. Either make a change or continue to think about it and suffer for the rest of your life. Always remember that sex is not the solution, for some men, it's the problem that is destroying us, women, children, families, homes, churches, and society as a whole. God is the solution to and for ALL things! Seek Him while He may be found.

# CHAPTER FIFTEEN

## "Creating Change"

Adjusting to change can be difficult, but some of us need to change our whole outlook or mind set. For the rest of us we need to rebuke the lies that we have been told. It is impossible to change when we are not only living a lie but believing it as reality. You might be wondering how you can change lies. It's simple, stop telling the lies and stop repeating the lies you have heard. We as men have to top allowing the lies to make us question our truth.

You see, the truth will always be a lie to you, unless someone tells you it's the truth. For example, how many people told you to follow your heart, and in the same sentence told you, as a man it's not good to express your emotions. If you really think about that for a minute, you will realize that makes no sense whatsoever. Let me break it down for you in case you are confused. When you follow your heart, where do you think your emotions come from? When you get emotional and cry, where do you think that comes from? When you get upset, should you not address your feelings? Of course, you should! But you need to think before you react to not make an emotional decision that could turn drastic.

But you still need to release what's in your heart. We all need to understand how to expose or address our emotions in the proper manner. I believe some of us do not know how to control or express our emotions, so we ignore, substitute, hide or act like they don't exist. We keep them in because we are told that feelings are for women. We are continually told that it's not cool to show our sensitive side. Don't cry in public. Don't communicate too much. Only women do that. I personally find it extremely funny when I see men humbled and exposed, including myself.

There are so many guys who look really strong outwardly, but inside are soft and weak. Unfortunately, we at times follow and focus on the wrong things. There are important times where we should focus on ourselves, then other times we should focus on others. Brothers we need to get our priorities straight. When it comes to other people, we tend to focus on *what they believe, who they know, how much money they have, how they got it, why not me, where can I get it, I didn't get it, life's a bi-ch, where is my money, I'm taking it, let's get high, let me hit that, it's not my kid, I don't want him around my son, where the party at, police brutality, where my lawyer at, bail me out, etc.*

Instead of focusing more on, getting the correct education, true spirituality, marriage, loyalty, getting in touch with our emotional side, being responsible for our kids, complete unity, being honest, becoming revolutionaries, etc.! I also believe that as men we sometimes have valid questions but have no answers. I honestly think we need to ask each other first before we can ask a stranger or a different culture the following questions:

*How do we truly feel deep inside?*
*What is truly bothering us?*

*Why do we view and treat women like trash?*

*Why do we fail to accept responsibilities as fathers?*

*Why do women put us on child support?*

*Why don't we really want another man around our child?*

*Why do we really get high or drunk most of the time?*

*Why as black men do department store executives frisk and question us more than any other color or culture?*

*Why are we more concerned about what party to go to on the weekend, than being concerned about spending time with our kids?*

*Why do we claim we don't trust anyone but are willing to follow illegal brainwashing religious rituals, gangs, etc.?*

Then we not only follow them but teach others to follow them as well. So, you tell me, who do you really trust? And why do you trust him, her, or them? You all want to teach, but are you really educated? If you are, then where did you get it from? Or better yet, how did you get it? This is the manual you want other men to follow. Are you serious? And speaking of following, who do you follow again? What is his name or practice? Furthermore, are you practicing what you preach? If the answer is no, then why? Do you even believe what you are being taught, should probably be the question?

I want men to stop hiding. The sad thing is you are really hiding from yourself. You are not getting to know yourself. We need to transform our minds and hearts in the right direction. We need to stop substituting our feelings, for false things. Our egos are not going to save us, instead they will get us in deeper trouble. Our outer pride is not going to protect us. Emotional suffocation is not the answer. Being afraid to feel is not the answer. Pretending that we are okay is not the answer. Just following our culture without knowing anything about it, is not the answer. Isolating ourselves from people and ourselves is not the answer. Being controlled by our insecurities is not the answer. I am a living witness that this does not work.

At one point in my life, I played basketball so much that I didn't realize it became my god. When I say god, I am talking about the time, energy, battles, commitment, and conviction that kept me focused on it and nothing else. I became devoted to basketball more than life itself. Nothing got in the way of me playing. If it was snowing, it didn't matter. I just waited until it was over, then I would shovel it away and get my basketball on. When I was grounded or disciplined it didn't matter. I created a basketball hoop out of a hanger and used a sock as the ball. Point is, nothing, I repeat nothing, got in the way of me focusing on basketball.

When I was down, discouraged, upset, or troubled, I ran to the Southside Jamaica Queens basketball court. I took out all of my frustrations on whoever would challenge me. When I was afraid to talk to girls it didn't matter to me either. That basketball named Spaulding was my beautiful girlfriend. She did exactly what I instructed and told her to do. She was very loyal and faithful, something that I could count on and always trust. It was my safe haven, my sanctuary that allowed me to expose and express myself emotionally and talent wise, so I thought.

This particular talent made me secure about my abilities as a baller, but it also gave me the confidence that that I desperately needed. But unfortunately, other things were still missing. I lacked balance due to my emotional anger. The pain that was still in me had not been addressed. By this time using basketball to push my pain and anger away became routine. You see, even though I grew up competitive, I didn't realize that I wasn't only competing against people, but I was competing at a higher level against myself.

I reached a point of no return. The end result was people being afraid of me on and off the court. I had so much anger in me without even realizing it. I thought people were intimidated by my skills, but they were intimated based off my anger. Little did I know these same people began to make fun and talk about my anger issue. I started getting into a lot of argumentative battles, but none of my friends would let me fight. A lot of them would always tell me, Charlie, or Rock, let the ball do the fighting for you. One day one of my close friends stopped and said, "Hey Charlie, do you realize what you are becoming?"

That very question made me realize that I was an emotional wreck! You see as I got older and more mature, I began to realize that there was life after basketball, and I needed to have something to fall back on. I needed something that I could look forward to and build within myself. At some point I started thinking I probably wouldn't make it as a professional baller. Do you understand me now? Most of my emotions were wrapped around basketball.

I begin to understand that I only expressed myself on the basketball court. I verbally communicated more on the basketball court, than I did off the court. I began to see the big picture about myself, and what I was to people. On the court I was a fearless basketball competitor, but off the court I was an emotionally insecure person. A lot of people always told me that I was a rock, and eventually that became my street name, C-Rock or Charlie-Rock. People looked up to me as Rock, someone who could face anything. A person that wouldn't let anything bother him or someone who could face any challenge. But little did they know I was insecure, lost, emotional, and inwardly crying.

Of course, there is a flip side to this story. In some way's basketball hurt me, but in other ways it helped me. Had I never realized I was good at something that required hard work, determination, passion, and perseverance I may have been more emotionally blocked. Basketball kept me out of trouble with people, but it got me in deep trouble with myself. In one aspect, it kept me from constantly thinking about my problems. In some form, it allowed me to release a lot of my pain. But you see, the problem started when I became too dependent on basketball and nothing else.

Inwardly, I was still very incomplete, or in a sense I was complete in one area, but incomplete, or insecure in another. I had low self-esteem in one area and had a big ego in another. The truth of the matter is, at times I didn't let anything bother me. I would overcome and get through any obstacle. I fought the toughest, ruthless, so called, or at the time, the "baddest" street hood gangsters, drug dealers, hustlers, you name it, I fought them all, and won most of the battles by myself. However, I was still lost, confused, and insecure. I still had a lot of catching up to do with myself, and my life. All of the battles and the street credibility on and off the court did not make me feel good inside.

Which brings me to my next question, my escape was basketball, “What is yours?” Men, what do you use to hide, ignore, substitute, or suppress the way you really feel? What is stopping you or causing you not to be open? What are you using as a shield to protect your true inner thoughts or emotional pain? Are you as, or more emotional as people say I was, because you choose to ignore your feelings through something or someone else? Please don’t answer me, instead take the time evaluate and get to know yourself?

# CHAPTER SIXTEEN

## "Born To Cry"

What is the first thing a baby does when he comes out of his mother's womb? You guessed correctly, he or she cries! Who teaches him or her how to cry? Where does the crying even come from? What causes the baby to cry, or what does it symbolize? And when does the crying stop?

Walk with me during this chapter, and let's answer these questions together. Let's start with the first question. The first thing a baby does is cry and, in my opinion, I believe it's because he or she was used to being in the womb. Being out of it for the first time might be scary or traumatic. Then when does the crying stop? Perhaps when the baby gets used to or adjust to his new life or environment. Now the other question is, where does the crying come from?

It comes from the baby's feelings or inner needs that he develops instantly. This is the ability and opportunity to express his feelings. Which we know have to come from the heart and soul, and soon the babies' mind, when it's fully developed. The baby learns for the first time how to express his feelings. He learns rather quickly that he gets attention this way and as time goes on, this is how he or she get there needs met.

The next question was, what does the crying symbolize? We already answered that. Remember, it's a form of expression. The baby is reaching out and getting the attention from whoever is listening, which is mostly likely a message to the mother or father.

**Crying** - *A Form Of Expression or Communication?*

This next topic is an extension of the above topic of a baby growing into a boy, while he continuously learns how to communicate through crying. I am going to start off by asking the question, and at the same time answering it. The question is, "Why does the baby continuously cry as he gets older?" Well, we all should know the answer to that question. It is the only way that he or she can express how it feels. It cannot communicate any other way, than to cry until it is taught how to talk.

Think about the baby automatically crying on its own, compared to him learning how to speak. Keep this particular thought in your mind while you meditate or concentrate on this topic. The mother or father, most of the time it's the mother by the way who has to learn how to recognize the signal and patterns of why the baby is crying. Eventually the parents will get to a point where they automatically know why the baby is crying.

They could be hungry, have a dirty pamper, something might be wrong physically, like stomach aches, might be tired, scared or upset. Or depending on how old they are, they might not like who is around them, because babies can pick up a bad vibe from people. As the child gets older, he or she starts to communicate differently; slowly but surely the baby stops crying as much; and of course, most of us wonder why? Well maybe because they start to express and establish their emotional feelings different; through communicating verbally.

Another reason might be parents, friends, and family members, starts telling the child to stop crying, and be tough. They say crying is for babies. So, what begins to happen is very obvious perhaps, the child begins to feel weird, ashamed, or even weak when he cries. He might feel like he needs to tough it out and be strong even though he is not fully aware of what being weak or strong means. This causes the child to slowly suppress or hide their feelings. Now of course, this goes back to the hold tough image, as well as the ego, and the outer pride crisis that the child begins to go through. Now let's back track.

The baby first felt comfortable crying in public out loud for any and every reason right! Now as time progresses, he slowly begins to cry behind closed doors, by himself. The only way he might cry outwardly is when he might see somebody else crying, not realizing that he is becoming a follower. He also doesn't realize that he is not only neglecting his feelings by being fake, but at the same time he is becoming a follower of the now established ego, instead of expressing or following his true self and becoming a leader of that same emotion. Now for this young individual, crying is not just an emotional thing, it becomes a psychological or mental thing.

And the repercussion and confusion is not just for the individual, it also affects the way the parent or guardian or people in general look at or raise their children. And of course, this can become an ongoing confusion not just for a family, but it becomes an ongoing cycle that is consistently taught in our society. This becomes a tug of war battle on whether to let the child cry or prevent him or her from crying to avoid any outer pride.

The young child is now taught to be strong, which is not necessarily a bad thing. However, it must be understood that crying doesn't means weakness. Crying does not have any bearing on whether the individual is strong or not. He needs someone to talk to or to figure out what is making him want to cry whether in public, behind closed doors, or deep within himself. This self-awareness will gradually allow him to understand and get to know who he is and what he will eventually be. And of course, this young man will slowly learn how to express himself in a way that he didn't even know was possible. This of course is what we call growth, perseverance, and maturity.

I believe a boy should determine his own maturity. Everyone doesn't mature the same way, or at the same pace. Some people like I said before, grow faster than others, some men are more emotionally in touch with their feelings than others. Now, I am not saying that a teenager, young man, or adult should go around crying every five minutes. But what I am saying is that no one should be forced to mature if or when they are not ready too. Think about this statement and at the same time, try to understand why I am using this illustration of the baby crying.

The first thing a baby does is cry. And he learns to cry on his own. I believe he should learn how to stop crying on his own as well. Do I believe that babies who cry most of the day should be handled in the same way as one who doesn't? No! It's just a matter of someone patiently finding out why he continues to cry so much. While slowly and wisely being careful not to make him feel weird, weak, too emotional, or not normal. Now here is where the pride comes in. I believe sometimes we as parents, are ashamed when our children cry more than normal. So, they want to stop him because, it is embarrassing to them or whoever is present.

My point is, just like a baby started crying on its own. It will stop on its own, as well, when he is ready to stop. It is just a matter of the child learning how to express his or herself to the point of it being healthy in a mature and balanced way without constantly crying to get attention or being spoiled. Some people are more sensitive than others; however, that doesn't necessarily mean something is wrong with them. It just means they are different. Once again society tells men, that we are not supposed to cry out loud in public, point is, most of us learned that at an early age. We are taught while we are too young to understand. Then later on we find that we weren't born feeling weak, suppressing feelings, and so on.

So, by the time we are adults we are already wired, trained, or mentally and emotionally programmed thinking that it's natural. Opposed to being forced or trained to be ashamed of our real and true emotions. This is good and healthy for the human soul, as long as it is controlled, released, and dealt with properly.

Society sometimes creates this false image for men. It teaches a man to hide his true feelings without recognizing the damages it is causing. These same men are ashamed if they don't do what society instructs them to do.

Final point is, most of all his life he has been told that crying is for girls. So, if he believes that, he will treat himself that way without noticing it, while rejecting his true self in the process.

**Society Battles** - *Concerning our emotions.*

A lot of men have told me that they don't go to funerals because they don't want to see the person that way. Which of course is understandable? However, they need to be careful that it's not because, they don't want to fully express themselves, or be seen crying and getting emotional in public. Most of the time when a man is hurt, sad, mad, or devastated, crying is the best thing he could possibly do. Simply because he is releasing all of the pain just like when he was a baby.

You cried when you got hurt. It's not a weak or strong thing, by which we are led to believe. Again, when you cried as a child, you got a response or reaction from someone, which let them see that you were hurt, sad, mad, distressed, or emotional. They were able to comfort you and help you. The same goes for a grown man.

Through studies, and intense research, most researchers and psychologist say that crying is good. So, in the same way, crying doesn't just help other people to comfort and support you, it helps you to comfort yourself, and release the emotional buildup inside of you. You are helping yourself when you release those tears. It causes your body to work properly. If you cry outwardly, someone will help you. Why because it's an innate emotion. A way to suggest that you need help.

Again, as a child if you didn't cry, how in the world would your mother and father know that something was wrong with you? They would think that everything is okay. As men we are sometimes afraid to feel, or sometimes afraid of our feelings, and even worst, to show how we feel. We are so busy worrying about how we look, or who is looking at us, rather than how we truly feel inside. As men we have to stop following this particular pattern of society and allowing it to define our manhood or how many times we cry in situations or circumstances.

My advice to all men is if you feel like crying, then CRY! You are going to always have feelings, whether you express them or not. Ladies, it's extremely dangerous for men to hide their feelings, especially towards you, kids, and life. Reason being, when the emotion eventually comes out, especially if its hidden pain; it will be in a negative way, causing more pain then intended. Now when I say negative, I mean in the form of verbal or physical abuse, as well as mental, due to these closed up feelings.

We need to learn how to express yet feel and understand them as well and that will take some time. But if we continue not to express them, that same time will be used and measured against us and destroy us, physically, mentally, emotionally, and sometimes spiritually if we don't express them at the right time.

**Genetically Speaking** - *Through Strong Studying, And Researching, On How Crying Is Actually Healthy For Us*

As I started to break down earlier, we as individuals must realize and understand what is healthy versus unhealthy. Believe it or not, crying is an extremely healthy way to release, and expose pain, sadness, bitterness, stress, agony, anxiety, and pressure. It is a help for you physically, mentally, emotionally, and definitely spiritually. But right now, I am mainly talking about the emotional, physical, and mental. Every time you cry, there is a form of emotional release that again, allows the body to operate normally.

In many areas, crying serves as a safety valve that allows your emotions to release built up pressure inside of you. This particular pressure in you will eventually cause different types of problems to your heart, which will cause major issues such as catharsis, which is a form of built up tension that is released and turns to purification. Catharsis is like what a shower is to the body, it cleans your insides just like a wash rag cleans your outsides (the body). Crying as we know also releases stress, depression, and sadness. All of the above need to be released daily if it enters the mind and body, regardless of the sex. Hint, Men! So far as we see, this is not just Charlie's opinion, this is more like a scientific fact.

To move further along, researchers are continually finding out more healthy ways to show crying is really a gift given to us by God. Sadly, some men choose not to use this gift because we are ashamed of it. However, in this case, our shame will cause us to put ourselves in negative emotional danger. Not realizing that this particular danger; even our pride and egos cannot help us. One of the reasons why we as men, don't see or understand this danger is because, it is hidden inside of us so that we nor others can see it.

For instance, someone who is stressful, upset, angry, or just flat out furious over a long period of time automatically builds up toxins and bacteria that will eventually damage the immune system, and hormones. This can lead to high blood pressure, anxiety, severe depression, panic attacks, ulcers, body aches, etc. Now the flip side to us crying out this particular pain results in, purification of the heart, peace in the mind, release of pressure, and a positive healthy attitude. It also kills bacteria in the eye lids and lowers personal magnesium levels, such as anxiousness, or stress, prevents small toxic molecules, restores the limbic system that is connected to the brain and some parts of the heart. Many of you are probably wondering why you didn't know this before. The word says it best, "lack of knowledge" which causes destruction.

We need to learn how to research on our own and educate others. So, if you didn't know it before, you know it now. Crying is a form of expression from the human body that was designed by God to protect us! And to be honest with you, I can go on and on and write many chapters on how powerful it is for the human body to shed these tears, but I won't, hopefully if you weren't educated before, now you have some idea. If still not convinced, I will leave you with a few more facts. Crying is cathartic, when you are hurt, the purpose of crying, is to break down, identify, and release the pain, with help from the brain, to clear, or expose the negative before it penetrates, spreads and affects your nervous and cardiovascular systems.

In other words, protect your inner system, and do not be deceived by societies system when it comes to crying. Learn how to protect your body from this stress. Remember that tears contain stress hormones that will protect the brain, and heart from any and everything it comes in contact with. Do you realize that crying is symbolic? For those of you who are really deep into this topic, or are reading carefully, you will begin to or will further understand how God sets us up to win at an early age.

This goes back to what you read earlier when I said that no one, or nobody can really explain how an infant is taught how to cry, although the definition is self-explanatory. God allows us to express ourselves through crying. The purpose is to cause our young bodies to be purified by the water that continuously keeps us healthy. But notice as we get older that same will of God becomes free will to us. We are now given the option to protect our body, emotionally, mentally, physically, and spiritually.

**The Brain And Heart** - *Working Together To Protect Our Emotional Pain*

You will soon read how this particular emotion becomes a routine by which continuously explains how the brain and heart becomes an advantage at times, while at other times becoming a disadvantage. I first realized this particular advantage helped me to understand, but at the same time become more grateful for both. It also allowed me to see the importance of the two and how they worked well together.

You can go through something so traumatic that you literally forget what happened! Amnesia! This is the brain and heart working together to protect the human soul from further suffering. And speaking of suffering, I was attacked, jumped, and beaten up by four individuals who had weapons, such as bats, poles, two by fours, pipes, etc. Outside of the physical suffering and abuse, there of course was emotional and mental suffering that I still go through today. Now here is the advantage and disadvantage. The advantage is, to this day I can't remember what happened.

I don't believe that I could even recognize the attackers if I saw them today. Now of course you may be asking, how not remembering what happened could be an advantage? Well, it depends on the person and how he or she deals with trauma. Now for me, because I was going through so much emotional pain or stress at the time, it caused me to block the emotional pain from my mind and heart.

Some might look at this as a disadvantage simply because I can't remember what happened. In some ways I can relate, in others I can't. The good bible as we call it simply says, "God does not give us more than what we can handle." Point is my spirit interceded and said enough is enough. Although it did not stop the violent attack, nor could it stop any other, at the same time it worked together with my mind allowing it to understand that it was too much for my heart to endure. With that being said, this allows me to be at peace with what happened to me to the point where I understand that I was being protected from myself.

My temper if it's triggered can and will destroy me faster than it can destroy anyone else. This of course is where the ego comes into play. My ego says, I fought all of them by myself with absolutely no fear in my heart. This is what people who were there told me, but of course not what I can remember. This same ego would make me continuously search or look for these individuals and not stop until I destroy them all.

And once again this allows me to be protected from the ego, or my outer pride that you learned about earlier. There is a huge difference when you try to protect or suppress your emotional embarrassment opposed to your spirit protecting your emotional pain that should be released. In this case, I didn't have to protect anything. My inner spirit combined with my brain and heart did it for me. Still in all, we all have to be incredibly careful, ready, able, and alert no matter what. Why? Because for whatever reason, the mind has the potential to turn against us.

Depending on the mindset of the person or situation, this is of course the very reason why we at all times need to release any type of discomfort, suffering, and pain in a positive way. Most men allow ourselves to be influenced by societies definition of how to handle our emotions. We at times ignore the message that the emotion is sending, meanwhile training ourselves to believe that feelings are meant to only be expressed with and through women.

This of course allows the mental to be separate from the heart, by which becomes deceived. So instead of these two key opponents being on the same page, they not only are on separate pages, but they are at the same time working and fighting against each other in a whole different book or in this case world.

When I say we are sometimes in a different world, I am mostly talking about in a fantasy or pretend world that we create in our heads concerning our emotions. I am talking about this world that we orchestrate, set up, and design for one another in this society that we are now influenced by. Some of us blame society not realizing that we are a part of the blame that we are complaining about.

# CHAPTER SEVENTEEN

## "Give Respect, Get Respect"

As men, we all want to be dealt with and treated with the utmost respect! We all know the famous saying, "Treat others as you would want them to treat you." And speaking of treating, I too once again had trouble with treating and dealing with women with the proper respect. So, I hope I am not coming of as a king, or a know how to treat women specialist, because I am not. Everything I am saying applies to me as well. So, I definitely need help sometimes, on how to respect, appreciate, love, and deal with women. Plus, also being able to manage my emotions when I feel like I am being disrespected by a woman. That was difficult for me, and sometimes still is. It's a learning experience that gets hard.

I slowly began to realize how bad or far off I was, when it came to loving a woman, when I started to be around them a lot. The more I was around them; the more I would get emotionally attached to them; which in my case was bad. Bad, because even though there was no more verbal name calling it became, I know it all. I call it, the I know it all syndromes. Come to Charlie's office syndrome. I will comfort, love, appreciate, honor, and respect you. Oh, he did what? He said what? He went where? How could he? And slowly but surely I became more attached to women issues, than my own.

I substituted, ignored, hid, and suffocated my emotional pain, with there's. A part of me back then felt sorry for a lot of women that was mistreated and called B's, hoe's, sluts, etc. So, I became this super savior, which is a title we used to be call in the hood. And once again my ego and outer pride was serious at this point. Because that title that I had in my mind, was serious enough for me to believe that I was different, like I was a real superhero to women or something. And during this time in my life (21-29) years of age, I got in a lot of trouble.

I over analyzed situations, was one sided, developed tunnel vision, had a big ego, was in uncompromising circumstances, became naive, was overprotective, and developed nothing but arrogance, and was full of pride. I thought I knew it all. To be honest, sometimes I still feel like I struggle with all of the above, with the exception of knowing it all. And some people might say, don't be so hard on yourself Charlie, your heart was in the right place. Correct, but where was my mind? Where was the wisdom behind it? It's almost like I had zeal with no knowledge.

I was basically fell for society's trap. I felt like I could take on the corruption, abuse, lies, and misleading of mankind, when it came to our society. I didn't really understand that I was only one person that needed a lot of help. And not just help concerning women, but help concerning men, and myself. I began to see the big picture. Not the big picture that society was creating concerning women, but the big picture of me that I was creating for myself.

And this became a very ugly picture. Like when you look at yourself in the mirror when you first wake up and you wish you could change it. Then I began to realize that in order for me to change that picture, I had to change my face. Then I began to realize that I was focusing too much on what the mirror showed me, than how I viewed myself. It wasn't what was on the outside of my face, THE FOCUS SHOULD HAVE BEEN ON, HOW DID I LOOK AND FEEL INSIDE, which caused me to see that I was only one person, who personalized, took on, or embedded too much on his heart and brain that overwhelmed his emotional connection to women.

As deep as that probably sound, it's really kind of simple. I became emotionally attached to women's heart, desire, compassion, needs, etc., because of the inconsistencies of men. I started to realize that it takes one man to corrupt many, and one man to expose them all, while including himself. Those mirrors helped me to see that I had to start off by looking at me, myself, and I. I began to realize that I was no better than the next man. I can't read about, write about, or fix no man, unless I fix myself. It's almost like I was crying out to myself through women, and they were doing the same to me.

It's not like we weren't helping each other, we just needed to help and get in touch with ourselves first. Which again allowed me to see that I can't be in nobody else business unless I fix and take care of my own. I could not save women or men, unless I saved myself. I couldn't take on the cares of society unless I took care of myself. I realized that I not only was disrespecting women, but I was disrespecting men and myself. I could not take good inner pride in myself because I was not respecting myself as a person. I ignored my feelings and replaced them with others. Sometimes we all can become selfish to ourselves and not even realize that we are the ones with the problems. I can't fix, help, or defend you if I can't defend myself. And as far as women, I also began to see that a lot of things that I did for women, they could have done it for themselves.

**Self-Respect** – Time for restoration.

As women, you can defend yourself by not calling each other a "B" as well. I know what you are probably thinking, come on Charlie, as women, it's a figure of speech. It's not that serious. Well okay, I understand your point. However, understand mines as well. All it takes is one figure of speech to spread throughout society that becomes a part of our daily use. You need to ask yourself; how would you feel if your young daughter, young sister, or niece was going around calling each other "B's". What if they were having the same or similar conversations that you are having with your friends, associates, or sisters?

The conversation goes like this, "When I grow up Shanice, I want to be a good "B", just like my mother, my aunt and my big sister. Then Rachel cuts her off and says, yeah Shanice me too. I am going to be a strong independent woman, not taking no bulls-t." Question women, how does that really sound and most importantly how does that make you feel?

Just think about the different slogans, or slangs, the figure of speech, or racial slurs that are disrespectfully destroying our neighborhoods, and at the same time building up traditional and cultural acceptance to our youth. They are accepting this word and are slowly redefining it through us. Children follow us as parents whether we believe it, like it, or not. The word bi-ch is not the only slogan or slang that they are following. I do not need to name them all. I'm sure you all know what I am talking about. You hear it and see it clearly each and every day.

Now let me break it down to you, from a man's perspective. When we hear you call each other b-ch, most of us men get excited while at the same time thinking that you accept it. Then we start thinking or constantly coming up with added slogans or street slangs to justify what the word means or represents for us towards you as women. And the funny but scary thing is, because there are so many women accepting and calling each other this word, we know in our hearts that for the few women who are against it, overall, it is a major argument and contradiction to women in general.

Believe me women, I know you all don't mean it the way sometimes us men do. You say it and mean what you say in a positive way. However, the word is still degrading, and its definition doesn't change, regardless of how much we repronounce it. Once this acceptance of the word is embedded in our minds, it's hard to delete the mental label or the conceptions of women and how to treat them in general. You all will time and time again disregard this fact, not realizing that some of you are disregarding the importance of the different ways, and levels that it is affecting the growing culture in our society concerning our youthful children.

And keep in mind that a child is innocent until he or she gets influenced and instructed by a guilty or popular tradition that's labeled to lead and teach to build the ego, increase the pride, expose the heart, and eventually misguide or mislead the soul. In this case, the soul is being taught by a society of people and not by its individual self. Of course, this is when the word being lost is not overused, but instead misunderstood or misinterpreted.

I believe that some men don't know just like I didn't what the "B" word even means. But we continue to use it simply because it's a popular word in our society that's false definition is nothing but a manmade street slang. Remember ladies that word started with one person making it popular. And in the same way one person or woman can change it to being unpopular as well. Whether it is a belief or not, we all know and see what this particular word or label has done in our society.

My bottom line is this, women respect yourself, and so will we. Tolerate disrespect, and the mam will disrespect you. Make a man respect everything about you, and he will surely catch on eventually. Play your role in changing the mindset of society, and so will we. Remember what you all tolerate and follow, so will your daughters, sisters, etc.

Kids feed off of us. Unfortunately, as you just read, they follow our lead as parents, good or bad. So please be examples for yourselves, and your children, especially your daughters, and allow your change, to change the way a man looks, and treat you as women.

A man will respect you, as much as you respect yourself. Respect is a long journey that we as men sometimes have to travel, consistently to overcome and get to. We sometimes get lost on the way. We need direction and a clear path that only a strong respectful woman can lead us to. We first have to clear our minds from any and all distractions. We have to know what we really want in our hearts, and if we really want you as our woman. Then we need to start up our engines and drive down the road of respect.

And if we need help, or are lost along the way, we know you women will show us the way. Hopefully, women, you all get my point. The way we treat you all, depends a lot on what you say, do, and act towards yourself. As women sometimes, you all have the GPS to our hearts and minds, because you all play a huge role in our lives. Solely at times it all depends on what you do, or say, how you act or react, or the way you treat and love you.

However, believe you me, I know a number of you who do not accept this title or word, this abuse and disrespect, the false definition of it, but still get mistreated. You find yourself still being disrespected, when some of you carry yourselves with a lot of class, integrity, and spirituality. This is not how you were taught. You were properly raised to do the right thing. Some of you waited until you got married and still ended up with the short end of the stick.

My charge to you is to continue to persevere, remain focused and strong, and get help if you are being forced to be or act in a way that is detrimental to you or your family. If you are continuously going back to that man that is threatening and abusing you, listen to me very carefully.

I would like to address to all you women out there, who accepts the abuse by men, whether it be verbal, mental, physical, or emotional. Do not continue to accept it! Do not tolerate it! Kill it, (not the man) before it kills you. Stop being in denial, reach out and get some help. Remove yourself from the situation. Regain your confidence and your self-respect. We suffer at times more than you all do. As men, some of us are crying for help through you all. We call you all "B's" because we are at times confused, and to a degree a lost follower trying to fit in and find our way, and of course this is not an excuse.

Some of us not only call you all "B's", but many could possibly feel like "B's" themselves. And of course, I am not talking about homosexuals, gays, or faggots to make that clear. I am not trying to disrespect them as well. Although, we at times are our own worst enemies that continuously lose ourselves. Most men who abuse are weak individuals, crying out and carrying out our pain on women. I say some of us are at times lost because our journeys are sometimes traps or dead ends.

Our paths are not straight, when all we do is abuse and call women "B's" all day simply because they may reject us. Here comes the confusion; we big up, follow and idolize men who we don't know and never met, and probably will never meet, meanwhile we put them up on a pedestal at times even when some of us might be fortunate enough to meet these individuals. A lot of us continuously get mad that we are not them, some of us are jealous of them because we simply don't have what they have, such as money, fame, glory, street credibility and so forth. To go a little further, for some of us who reach our goals, accomplish what we strive for, and are indeed satisfied, it somehow blinds us to what type of hidden insecurities we might have had before we became successful, before we had that beautiful queen.

Sometimes what happens is that beautiful queen, in and out, becomes the bi-ch that we created within ourselves. We start to do and say all types of disrespectful things to women or our woman, but slowly begin to treat our male friends like kings. This is when the woman that has been there for you so long begins to realize that she is not and was never the problem. She begins to realize that something is really internally wrong with her man. Her thinking goes like this, "How can he treat a man, who is just like him good, but treat his woman, who slaves for him, and treats him like a king bad?"

You get into a fight or argument with your so called man, two weeks later, you break bread with him, and you all are cool again. On the other hand, you beat on, cheat on, disrespect, abuse, accuse, embarrass, and humiliate your woman, who you consistently refer to as a bi-ch, day after day, week after week, month after month, and year after year. Come on women, wake up! If that's your man, I repeat, he's lost, and so will you be unless you stay away from him. If he doesn't get help, leave him. If he is consistently abusing you then his path is not clear, and his road is going to lead to destruction because he is self-destruction within itself.

Once again, if you love yourself and him, then get him some help, and be patient with his process, make sure you are being counseled as well. If things don't change, then respect yourself enough to leave. If you stay with him, then you will wear that name and live it, and he will feel comfortable calling you his "bi-ch" while treating you like the true definition as well.

Now check out this particular woman. This is the independent woman, not bi-ch, but the independent woman that you describe to your coworkers, your friends, your daughters, as possibly your future fiancé or wife. A real man would have no choice but to appreciate, respect and love such a woman like this, who has personality, charisma, character, dignity, class, and that can take the good inner pride in herself that no title or name can take away.

Please women don't follow the cultured society that was created by such a word, follow, and lead yourself to build and create your own image of what a true woman should be in a new society that you repaired and led to complete perfection in your own words. Still in all you might have some cases where you are doing exactly what you are supposed to do as a woman, you are being independently strong, leading your family in a positive way, but the problem is you have a boyfriend, fiancée or husband that is not following your example. You are basically leading the family and trying to lead him at the same time. This is when the problems and the confusion arise.

I Charlie Merriweather once again thought in my mind that I was different from everybody else, while hoping at the same time to set myself apart. At the age of 18 is when I felt the need to start and be a part of a group or gang called *The Lost Souls*. I am sure this name alone allows you to think or understand how lost, or confused I really was. Still in all, that name "Lost Souls", fit who, what, and where I was at the time, lost! Of course, now I understand that this was my soul crying out for help. The rest is self-explanatory, but to elaborate and make my point of course I have to go a little further! Me and some of my peers formed this particular group called "THE LOST SOULS."

This particular group started out with about 15 people in the beginning, probably reaching to the point of like 100 people deep and counting. We weren't really a well-known gang like the Crips and the Bloods or anything like that. But we were well known in our neighborhood. We were definitely well established and recognized in our community. Keep in mind though, we were not a group that beat people up, sold drugs, robbed people, or did anything like that.

With that being said, you might ask so why then did we form or start this group? The answer is, we followed at that time, what our neighborhood or society influenced and showed us. Everybody else, who was so called about something, was a part of some click. So just in case, a particular group, gang, or crew, wanted to challenge us, we wanted to be unified and well prepared to defend ourselves collectively. After going through a lot of challenging experiences with people, ourselves in the group, and various other groups, we individually started to split with of course me being the first to leave, after 2 years as a member.

After that others followed, it was like a domino effect. Our group lasted about three more years until eventually everyone split. Now my reason for leaving at the time that I did back in 1995, I felt in my heart that I was no longer lost. I began going to church and reached a point where I could no longer have a title with such a name as the *lost souls*. Common sense will tell anybody whether they are religious or not that your souls supposed to be saved in church, not lost; so, I thought!

In my mind I found God and He saved my soul, I was no longer lost but was simply the opposite, saved. At last, in my spirit, mind, heart and soul, I was saved from the streets of society. So that meant that my title, label, and associated name had to change from a *lost soul to a saved soul*.

Shortly after I quit, the group dismantled. This brings me to my next point. I realized that I became or was becoming a follower, and that I had a follower's mentality. It took me getting closer to God, for me to realize that I didn't need to be a part of any group, click, or gang association, to feel protected or to fit in. What does it take for other men to see that that's not the way to go? Does someone have to die, that you are close to? Does someone have to scare the living daylights out of you, in order for you to change your mind set? Does your child have to follow your lead, for you to understand how serious the influence the streets or society have on us at times?

By now you are probably wandering, what does this have to do with calling a woman a "B". And my answer will be this, how many times have you heard the saying, "Life's a bi-ch!" Do you understand me now? A lot of men follow that mentality. I can speak for every member in the lost soul group, we all before we joined that group believed that life was a bi-ch, and that it was kicking us in the you know what. So, we believed that we had to fight life back. At some point in the life of a teenage boy growing into a man, he will feel as if life is a bi-ch. So, in believing that, we treat life in that manner. We treat women that way, and then they treat themselves that way.

If a man feels like life is a bi-ch, he is saying that most of the times, life sucks. Which means it's not fair. It's a lot of unfortunate or negative situations, or circumstances that are bad. So, in a lot of our minds, we feel or come to the notion that life treated or is treating us bad. So now we feel like life owes us something which is incorrect. I believe we owe it to ourselves to be something, or somebody, to be successful. I agree that life has its challenges. Believe you me, some are frustrating, depressing, difficult, and stressful. But there are some good things life has to offer as well, such as "beautiful women." Granted, you do have some women who are lost, confused, rude, ghetto, prideful and brainwashed. This still does not mean they should be labeled as bi-ches.

It means that they have issues that need to be addressed. In the same way, we sometimes think, or say life's a bi-ch while making it about the women in our lives. That mentality is unbelievably bad to have.

Why, because, we treat women the same way we treat life, because they fit our definition on this topic. Just like we feel like life owes us something, we feel the same way about them. We put life and women in the same negative, degrading category at times and start to treat both of them the same.

If a woman is weak, we as men need to encourage them to be strong. If they are lost, then we need to educate them to be saved. If they are down, then we need to lift or pick them up. We are here to lead, not to follow. The only thing we need to follow is, what's right, respectful, and true. The truth lies in us, it begins with all of us men having the right mindset. God created us with beautiful minds. He doesn't want them to be wasted, or corrupted. The saying is true, "A mind is a terrible thing to waste." And guess what! So is a good woman. Believe me, there are more good women than there are bad. And men, if you don't agree with me, then just think about it for a minute. If you have a woman, and you are with them, and you refer to them as "B's" then what does that say about yourself or show who you are. Thank you, I rest my case!

WOMEN, please stop repeating this awful statement, "A man is going to be a man!" I understand what you are referring too. When we mess up, blow it, or make the same so called mistakes, again, again, and again. However, first think about what you are saying to us before you say it, though!

When you say a man is going to be a man, you are putting all of us in the same category. And what it does is, opens the door for us to continue to be unfaithful to you, abuse you, lie to you, commit adultery, trap you with more kids, put you in the system, and the list goes on and on. But to continue my point, when you tell us that we are going to continue to be the way we are regardless, you are giving us a free get out of jail pass to further say that we can't help who we are, which means that you all should accept it, and not expect us to change, because we can't, right!

Then we flip the script and begin to complain and say, women call us dogs by which is the opposite of who they are, female dogs. Are you beginning to see what I mean? We can easily reverse it back at you all and at the same time allow our society to understand that you woman have double standards and are furthermore contradicting yourselves. This is how both of the respected sexes (male and female) become two victims of society that of course was created by us. In this case, we try our hardest to turn the negative degrading word into a positive traditional and cultural thing.

So, remember women, don't add to a man's ignorance, by being ignorant yourselves. Love honor and respect yourselves by not allowing us to disrespect you all. I believe all women are special in God's eyes. As men we need to look at women the same way. I believe the only way that we can collectively look at them the way God does, is if, we look at ourselves, and find ourselves through God!

# CHAPTER EIGHTEEN

## "A Few Good Men"

I'm sure you have heard the classic cliché, "All men are the same or all men are dogs!" I will be truthful most men possess similar characteristics and can be disrespectful towards women. But this is NOT, and I repeat NOT the same for ALL men. There is still "A Few Good Men" left in the world. To be totally honest, I believe there will be more good men, when we are willing to do what I have done through this book and that is tell the truth. Like I have stressed over and over again, we have the power to educate one another to make our lives better which will create a positive dynamic in the world around us.

I have learned that I can do better and be better when I know what better looks like. Some men get stuck at certain places in their lives because they didn't have the proper example. As boys growing up, we were told not to cry because it made us look weak, but why would God give us tears if they were not meant to be used. Now you may have grew up in a house where the father was always mean mugging or had that deep base in his voice, you know that get right tone. Which means he never let you see him sweat. If he cried, which I'm sure he did, it was probably in the car on the way home from a stressful day at work. Maybe he cried in the restroom while taking a shower.

The point is you never saw it, therefore, this justifies the theory that men don't cry. Well, God chose "a few good men" that cried during the battles, trauma, pressure, and trials of their lives. These were powerful men who understood the importance of shedding tears while crying out to God. These men endured hardships we probably could never face. Which brings me to Brother David, Jesse's son, who was tending the sheep and minding his business before he was chosen to become a king by God.

He was a normal ordinary boy who grew into a man just like you and me. He didn't have any superpowers that caused him to be great. He acted out of his emotions and made dumb choices regarding women just like you and me. David cried out to God on numerous occasions, mostly because of what he was turning into. Once he became king, that old ego started kicking in and he found himself operating in the flesh. He was highly anointed in the spirit and favored by God, but every now and then the flesh part of him made himself known. He found himself in drastic situations that only God could get him out of.

David was special to God because he knew how to humble himself. He didn't have a problem with showing his emotional side. The bible says he danced before God until his clothes came off. This brother lost himself in the Lord. God called him the apple of his eye, but that apple started getting rotten at some point. He started dealing with the spirit of lust, which led to deceit, betrayal, murder, and the loss of a child. David wanted Uriah's wife so bad he intentionally put the man on the front line of war to ensure he would be killed. That's some shady stuff!!

Now the difference between many men and David is that we would allow pride to make us think we are right. David knew he was wrong, so when the baby was born sick, he fell on his face and wept before the Lord. Praying and asking God to save the baby, but God said no. My point is even though David sinned before God, he didn't run from God, he ran to God. He understood that God was loving, forgiving, and compassionate towards him. Just think how much better your life would be as a man, if you adopted the principles and the characteristics of David.

What I mean is David cried out to God as a sinner like me and you, but still was answered by God. It is not a coincidence that crying and dying to the old self pleased God. David was a man that was slowly dying spiritually because of sexual sin. So, before he died physically, he had to emotionally reconnect with God in his heart, in order to be mentally alert and stable. God rewarded him with a new heart of change, joy, and a deep emotional and spiritual connection that sin could not break. Sounds like being saved to me!

Let's go deeper and check out some other "real men" who cried!!! Brother Esau in Genesis 27:38 said to his father, "Do you have only one blessing, my father? Bless me too, my father! Then Esau wept aloud." This man was hustled out of his birthright by his own brother and mother. Come on that is enough to shed a couple of tears. The bible tells us that our enemies will be those of the same household. The list of men continues!

**Genesis 29:11**

*Then Jacob kissed Rachel than began to weep aloud.*

**Genesis 33:4**

*But Esau ran to meet Jacob and embraced him; he threw his arms around his neck and kissed him. And they wept.*

**Genesis 45:14**

*Then he threw his arms around his brother Benjamin and wept, and Benjamin embraced him, weeping.*

**Genesis 50:17**

*This is what you are to say to Joseph: I ask you to forgive your brother's the sins and the wrongs they committed in treating you so badly. Now please forgive the sins of the servants of the God of your father. When their message came to him, Joseph wept.*

**2 kings 29:19**

*Because your heart was responsive and you humbled yourself before God when you heard what he spoke against the place and its people, and because you humbled yourself before me and tore your robes and wept in my presence, I have heard you, declares the Lord.*

**2 Samuel 19:1**

*Joab was told, "The King is weeping and mourning for Absalom.*

***2 Kings 8:11***

*He stared at him with a fixed gaze until Hazel felt ashamed. Then the man of God began to weep.*

***Job 16:20***

*My intercessor is my friend as my eyes pour out tears to God.*

***Psalm 6:8***

*Away from me, all you who do evil, for the Lord has heard my weeping.*

***Isaiah 33:17***

*Look, their brave men cry aloud in the streets, the envoys of peace weep bitterly.*

***Isaiah 38:5***

*Go and tell Hezekiah, This is what the Lord, the God of your father David, says: I have heard your prayers and seen your tears; I will add fifteen years to your life.*

***Matthew 26:7***

*Peter weeps after Jesus told him he would betray him.*

***Philippians 3:18***

*Paul weeps for the Church in Philippi.*

***Ezra 10:1***

*While Ezra was praying and confessing, weeping.*

***Luke 19:41 and John 11:35***

*Talks about how Jesus wept over the City and for Lazarus.*

I have shared sixteen instances in the word of God where MEN wept. The last two I shared tells us that even Jesus cried. He cried because of the condition of the city and He cried because His friend died, the same friend He resurrected. I'm almost certain that He knew He would be performing a miracle that day, but He was human. How many men do you know that will cry over the condition of their community?

We as men need not to be ashamed, for the simple fact that some of the most powerful men who were Kings, Apostles, Judges, etc., all cried out to God or to their loved ones in the bible. These men had to cry out their pain, suffering, shortcomings, and rejections, all to get closer to themselves and God. If you continue to read books on emotions, as well as the bible, you will begin to understand more that crying outwardly is a form created by God that will allow us to release ourselves inwardly to be healed.

The prophet Jeremiah was labeled as "The Weeping Prophet." This was the same man that God declared to be a Prophet, which had a fortified city, an iron pillar, and a bronze wall. Just like Tupac said, "This POWERFUL man was known to SHED SO MANY TEARS!" Too many men suffer in silence by hiding our pain from people and ourselves. Crying can prevent further damage from the pain that was originally caused. This is an expression from the heart, by which God looks at, that will guide and allow you to be strong, without anything that the soul can hide. Which in reverse, if you do hide your pain, and if you feel like you want to cry, but you don't, you will slowly die to who you really are, and won't get the help you need to release what's meant to be released in the first place.

If you have to cry, then cry. It's the same as, if you have to laugh, you laugh. Both are emotions that should equally be expressed. For example, a doctor might tell you, if you have high blood pressure from worrying, sometimes being in an atmosphere or environment, that allows you to laugh is good and can lower your pressure. Therefore, he might tell you to stay around people that are humorous, funny, that uplifts and brings joy to your heart.

What is joy? Joy is being at peace with God, yourself, and whatever circumstance, tragedy, or situation you might be in. You see, happiness is really a part of the feeling, that's depending solely on the state of the situation, or predicament. That's why some people say they are happy today, and tomorrow they might say they are sad or miserable. Or let me use a more detailed common example. When you are in a good relationship, you are happy. But if you break up the relationship, for whatever reason, you become sad. Sad because the relationship has ended.

We as men need to be reborn to ourselves. By doing this, we will not be brainwashed, or misled, by the evil desires of this world. This will allow us to get even closer to God, as we get closer to who we really are. This will reveal and educate us to distinguish the truth from a lie, and speaking of truth, this will allow us to be truthful to who we are with, or around, to the point where we will be introduced, recognized, and identified as leaders, and not followers. We will no longer get emotionally upset, or painfully deceived sexually, to the point where we get addicted to it, and not committed and loyal to the woman.

Women will no longer identify us as deadbeats, abusers, or liars, but identify us as truthful, faithful, and committed fathers. We will be fathers who are no longer influenced, enticed, or dragged away by drugs and alcohol, but are saved and led by God's Holy Spirit. The same spirit that will uplift, encourage, take care of, and build us up in every way possible to teach, instruct, restore, and create a society that's designed by real men. To make this revelation a reality we must first die to our old selves daily. We must intentionally choose to live free and joyful. Soul searching will take the heart to a peaceful place that the mind will recognize to secure and prepare the individual for the spirit to intercept the love of God.

That is my hope for every human being, especially for every man that will walk this earth. The hope is for everyone to get in touch with who they are and to understand that *men cry too...* "Real Men." Brother if you have to shed tears, then do it, don't substitute, suffocate, or be ashamed. God will turn those tears, to tears of joy at the right time. Believe me, the right time is now!! Why, because no one is guaranteed tomorrow.

***Poetic Flow***

*For all the men who push, but don't stop these kids, who don't sell, or shop these kids, who don't fail to watch these kids, who don't run, but adopt these kids, don't mistreat, but respect these kids, who don't beat, but protect these kids, who don't leave, or neglect these kids, who don't forget, or regret these kids, who don't mislead, but direct these kids, who are not afraid, but correct these kids, who will teach, and elect these kids, I have nothing but praise, to all men who accepts these kids?*

This final chapter is solely dedicated to all the men who are walking the walk and talking the talk. This chapter is for all the mature men, who are persevering, striving, and fighting to be strong, and powerful, no matter the circumstance or situation. For all the men who are beating the odds in this evil world, to be powerful successful men. I big up all my peoples who are incarcerated for no reason. For those who are innocent, but were, indicted for crimes you didn't commit, but are still doing their time like troopers.

My heart goes out to men like you. My soul reaches out to men like you. My spirit cries out to men like you. I wish it were more men like you. I want to continue to shout out to all my brothers, who don't run from the responsibility of raising his son or daughter correctly. Who help out the mother of his child, regardless of the nature of their relationship? For all the men who marry these beautiful women with kids that are not there's but still treat them like they are.

I also want to shout out to all the men who accept the responsibility that God has given them. For all of you, who answer the tears and cries of God's children? I got nothing but respect and love for all of you. I have nothing negative or bad to say about anyone of you. I have nothing but good to say about you.

***Poetic Flow***

*Even though we all fail, continue to strive for protection, continue to look for God's protection, you always will prevail, when you are guided by God's direction, you will never have to tell, or live a lie, to defend a question, don't get discouraged show the affection from your heart continue to try, to live your life for God's correction, before things fall apart, He is with you wherever you will go, He is with you to help you to grow, To turn your back on God, is not very smart, are you now feeling the poetic flow, that God put in my heart, Do you now no, that you was being that example from the very start, you have now learned, now it's time to teach the lesson, and appreciate the beautiful art, and that is the art to love, the art to feel, the start to love, what is real, the real responsibility to strive to be men like you, who are in the image of God, although to a fake man, it doesn't appeal, and is very odd.*

I want to give praise and shout out all my *peoples* who are oversees getting that money to support their families. To all of you men, who are working two to three jobs to make ends meet? For all of you who are living check to check to pay your rent, or mortgage on a house that's realistically not even yours. But are still faithful and committed to your families, and not even complaining. God is watching, He will take and bring you back from poverty and captivity.

I want to continue to shout you out for being loyal and faithful to those special women every single day, regardless of what the next man is doing. I have nothing but praise for the man who doesn't blame the white man for his shortcomings and failures. I have enough respect for the men who are not prejudice, but respect and accept every man, regardless of color.

I have nothing but respect for the man who unfortunately raises his daughter or son alone. My heart goes out to men like you. My soul reaches out to men like you. My spirit cries out for men like you. I wish it were more men like you.

I have nothing but respect and love for all the men who were raped, abused, molested, mistreated, abandoned, tortured, brainwashed, forgotten, and left for dead, but still overcame it, got help for it, rose above it, and who didn't use these painful things, as an excuse to do it to someone else.

For all of the men who got stronger because of it, who grew because of it, he can, and is teaching now, because of it. Who became students of God because of it? Who got in therapy because of it? And who are now better, strong, powerful men because of it.

I encourage you men, continue to fight, continue to search, continue to restore, and continue to take great pride in who you are. You have nothing to be ashamed of. But have everything to be proud of. My heart goes out to men like you, my spirit cries out to men like you, my soul is proud of men like you, I wish it were more men like you.

I also want to big up, and shout out, and encourage all the men who lost their father's, mother's, or any family member, and got stronger because of it. Continue to keep your head up my *peoples,* allow their legacy to live on through you. I feel your pain, I lost my mother, and grandmother, accept my condolences, prayers, and inspiration. Hopefully, they are or will be in a better place than we are. Make them proud of you, as if they are still here.

Continue to be strong, cry if you have to, release your pain in a positive way, persevere, allow yourself to take it higher, don't be, or add to the problem like some of us do, understand that it's not our problem to solve, understand that it's really not even a problem. Believe and understand that it's life, and it's everybody's fate someday. Meanwhile, find and fulfill your purpose if you already haven't, and conquer this earth.

Understand and focus on the real problem, try to figure out, why aren't there enough men like you. Go far, move on, and accomplish your dreams, and make them a reality! Remember and realize that those special memorable moments that you have, will never be lost, but there are so many people who are.

I appreciate men like you, I look up to men like you, my heart goes out to men like you, my soul reaches out to men like you, my spirit can relate to men like you, I wish it were more men like you.

## ***Poetic Flow***

*To all the men who push other men to be successful, who don't just take, but give something special, who are not fake, but live, and are not stressful, They don't just listen, but react, and respond, they don't just say, but they do what's respectful, to establish or create that deep bond, the bond of peace, that will never decease, that's always write, but never wrong, that allows his love, to always increase, like a special song, that will always believe, and forever belong, so continue to achieve, be confident and remain faithful and strong, I Charlie Merriweather can go on and on and on, because spiritually speaking my soul will always live and move on and on and on.*

I want to continue to shout out all the men who stand out, or stand up for what they believe in, regardless of how it looks, regardless of who's there, regardless of the support they get, regardless of how they are perceived. Regardless of how they sound. Men continue to be strong, educate you, and continue to lead, follow no man, trust, and serve God only. Stay focused, eliminate all kinds of deceitful distractions, be of great courage, don't let anyone look down on you, walk with your head high, look at men eye to eye, keep your paths straight, don't allow your wisdom to be scorned by fools.

Always remember that bad company corrupts good character. So, remain humble and mind your own business, and allow your business to be minded by you. Keep your circle small, unless it is surrounded by Godly influences. Still watch out for the antichrist and the imposters, who don't practice what they preach. God is watching you, He will instruct, protect, guide, and lead you in the right direction, if you seek Him. God is your biggest fan. He is your biggest support, and really all the support you need. He will do all He can to keep you away from the evil one, and the fire. God is the number one master plan, that will never expire, don't follow the deceitful one, who doesn't have a plan, and is called a pathological liar.

God is glad He made men like you. God is watching men like you. God will save men like you. God has a home for men like you. I wish it were more men like you. Speaking of God, I want to commend and shout out all the men who have and are striving to have a personal relationship with God. I look up to the men who don't think it's weak or whack to have a relationship with their creator.

For all the men who listen to God's Holy Spirit. For all the men who understand God's plan for their lives. I want to shout out all the men who are faithful Christians, real preachers, who follow God regardless of religion, who preach the truth, real pastors who guide, instruct, and lead people, real ministers of reconciliation, real men who really love people and God regardless of their title, stats, devotion, or worship.

I also want to thank all of the great men of faith in my life, Leo Siffliet, Kendall Knight, Charles Merriweather Sr, Gene, Jarriel Merriweather, Robert Jones, Reggie Wilson, Virgil, Ralah Mc'nair, Tone, Jamel Horton, Yohance, Apostle Larry King, Pastor Kevin, Cyril Staley, and Sharad Stevenson. Thank you all for inspiring me, understanding, and believing in me. My heart goes out to men like you. My soul responds to men like you, my spirit rejoices with men like you, I wish it were more friends like you.

I want to also shout out all the men who were told that they are failures, dumb, illiterate, retarded, uneducated, ugly, weird, slow, crazy, stupid, a waste of life, never going to make it, not talented, turned back because of color, etc., and proved all these foolish people wrong.

You have persevered and stood your ground. Continue to be successful and grow. Continue to be true to who you are, my *peoples, my brothers,* you have nothing else to prove. Your gift, talent, and success speaks for itself. You speak for the life that you live. You speak for the heart that you have. You speak for the soul that you are. You speak for the man of God that's in you!!...

## ***Poetic Spiritual Flow***

*With that being said, continue to show it, don't hide it, don't blow it, please provide it, don't you know he will guide it, don't you know he will find it, you will grow behind it, don't fast forward or rewind it, go towards, but not behind it, it's your reward, that designs it, can you afford to decline it, do you need more time to find it, will you bleed before you find it, or will you sign your life away, do you know what to say, do you know how to pray, is it your seed that shined it, would you get on your knees every day, is your heart behind it, you still don't know what to say, you still can't find it, God will show you the way if you yield to His Holy Spirit, and you will eventually win, and be called one of the Few Good Men.*

God made us all in His image, so we as men are all blessed by God, so God bless you, or better yet, may He continue to bless us all.

Remember...REAL MEN CRY!!!!!!!!!!

# SPECIAL TRIBUTE

## "My Four Brothers"

*Kaheen Wilson*
*Cisco Vandenberg*
*Will Smith (not the actor)*
*Apostle King Larry Crawford*

To be honest I don't know where to begin, so let me start by saying that I honor and love each one of you individually as well collectively. Proverbs 18:24 says, "A man of many companions may come to ruin, but there is a friend who sticks closer than a brother." This is a true word that describes each one of you – men who have been closer than a brother to me. When I think back over my life and the roads I had to travel, I thank God that He allowed our paths to cross. I thank God that He created you and divinely connected me with such amazing men.

Each one of you are vastly different, but each one of you played a similar role in my life. It was your wisdom, knowledge, understanding, patience, virtue, and truth that helped to shape and build my character as a man. I appreciate your honesty when I needed it the most. I appreciate that you didn't let me sink or swim alone. I can honestly say that I have always felt safe and protected as your brother and even though I am expressing these words, this still is not enough.

I appreciate the fact that each one of you were willing to open up and give your heart and not simple word service. Each one of you showed up with action when I called and knew to be there when I didn't call. I have gained so many valuable things from each one of you that will continue to carry me on this journey called life. I pray that I have been half as much of a brother as you have been to me.

Thank you for sharing in my dreams, my goals, my visions, and my aspirations. Thank you for pushing me when I didn't want to be pushed. Thank you for being patient when I didn't want to listen. Thank you for never giving up on me. Thank you for true brotherly love. You will always hold a special place in my heart as I pray for you and your families daily. I speak blessings over your life and may the favor of God always locate you for the seeds you have sown in my life.

In addition, I would like to also acknowledge Ronald Ulysses, Raheem Wiggins, and my boy Evans Traynham.

Much love,
Your Brother Charlie

# AUTHOR BIO

## "Charles Merriweather"

Charles Merriweather, aka "Pastor Majestic" is a man who loves and honors God for the blessings and favor that He has bestowed upon his life. Born a native of Queens, New York, Charles has experienced many ups and downs, but through the grace of God he persevered and strives today to walk in his purpose.

Charles is an ordained pastor, a writer of prophetic poetry, and a motivational speaker. He worked for the Department of Education for twenty-six years. His favorite things to do are play basketball and go to the movies. He chooses to spend quiet time with God during his prayer walks and reading and studying his bible.

As an ordained pastor Charles will be starting a ministry called "Spiritual Truth Ministries." He is currently a member of "We Got The Power International Ministries." Charles also serves as a state certified chaplain. Charles has several upcoming ventures which include an upcoming gospel show and two additional books.

**Contact Information**
Email: realmencrybook@gmail.com
Website: www.charlesmerriweather.com
Facebook: @charles.merriweather